IMMERSION
Bible Studies

MATTHEW

Praise for IMMERSION

"IMMERSION BIBLE STUDIES is a powerful tool in helping readers to hear God speak through Scripture and to experience a deeper faith as a result."
Adam Hamilton, author of *24 Hours That Changed the World*

"This unique Bible study makes Scripture come alive for students. Through the study, students are invited to move beyond the head into the heart of faith."
Bishop Joseph W. Walker, author of *Love and Intimacy*

"This beautiful series helps readers become fluent in the words and thoughts of God, for purposes of illumination, strength building, and developing a closer walk with the One who loves us so."
Laurie Beth Jones, author of *Jesus, CEO* and *The Path*

"I highly commend to you IMMERSION BIBLE STUDIES, which tells us what the Bible teaches and how to apply it personally."
John Ed Mathison, author of *Treasures of the Transformed Life*

"The IMMERSION BIBLE STUDIES series is no less than a game changer. It ignites the purpose and power of Scripture by showing us how to do more than just know God or love God; it gives us the tools to love like God as well."
Shane Stanford, author of *You Can't Do Everything . . . So Do Something*

IMMERSION
Bible Studies
MATTHEW

J. Ellsworth Kalas

Abingdon Press

Nashville

MATTHEW
IMMERSION BIBLE STUDIES
by J. Ellsworth Kalas

Copyright © 2010 by Abingdon Press

Library of Congress Cataloging-in-Publication Data

Kalas, J. Ellsworth, 1923-
  Matthew / J. Ellsworth Kalas.
    p. cm. -- (Immersion Bible studies)
  ISBN 978-1-4267-0982-1 (perfect binding : alk. paper)
  1. Bible. N.T. Matthew--Textbooks. I. Title.
  BS2576.K35 2010
  226.2007--dc22
                    2010026841

**Editor: Jack A. Keller, Jr.
Leader Guide Writer: Mark Price**

10 11 12 13 14 15 16 17 18 19—10 9 8 7 6 5 4 3 2 1

Manufactured in the United States of America

Contents

REVIEW TEAM

Diane Blum, Pastor
East End United Methodist Church
Nashville, Tennessee

Susan Cox, Pastor
McMurry United Methodist Church
Claycomo, Missouri

Margaret Ann Crain
Professor of Christian Education
Garrett-Evangelical Theological Seminary
Evanston, Illinois

Nan Duerling
Curriculum Writer and Editor
Cambridge, Maryland

Paul Escamilla
Pastor and Writer
St. John's United Methodist Church
Austin, Texas

James Hawkins
Pastor and Writer
Smyrna, Delaware

Andrew Johnson
Professor of New Testament
Nazarene Theological Seminary
Kansas City, Missouri

Snehlata Patel, Pastor
Woodrow United Methodist Church
Staten Island, New York

Emerson Powery
Professor of New Testament
Messiah College
Grantham, Pennsylvania

Clayton Smith, Pastoral Staff
Church of the Resurrection
Leawood, Kansas

Harold Washington
Professor of Hebrew Bible
Saint Paul School of Theology
Kansas City, Missouri

Carol Wehrheim
Curriculum Writer and Editor
Princeton, New Jersey

IMMERSION BIBLE STUDIES

A fresh new look at the Bible, from beginning to end,
and what it means in your life.

Welcome to IMMERSION!

We've asked some of the leading Bible scholars, teachers, and pastors to help us with a new kind of Bible study. IMMERSION remains true to Scripture but always asks, "Where are you in your life? What do you struggle with? What makes you rejoice?" Then it helps you read the Scriptures to discover their deep, abiding truths. IMMERSION is about God and God's Word, and it is also about you—not just your thoughts, but your feelings and your faith.

In each study you will prayerfully read the Scripture and reflect on it. Then you will engage it in three ways:

Claim Your Story
> Through stories and questions, think about your life, with its struggles and joys.

Enter the Bible Story
> Explore Scripture and consider what God is saying to you.

Live the Story
> Reflect on what you have discovered, and put it into practice in your life.

IMMERSION makes use of an exciting new translation of Scripture, the Common English Bible (CEB). The CEB and IMMERSION BIBLE STUDIES will offer adults:

- the emotional expectation to find the love of God
- the rational expectation to find the knowledge of God
- reliable, genuine, and credible power to transform lives
- clarity of language

Whether you are using the Common English Bible or another translation, IMMERSION BIBLE STUDIES will offer a refreshing plunge into God's Word, your life, and your life with God.

1.

The Birth of Jesus

Matthew 1–2

Claim Your Story

Think back for a few moments about how you first learned the Christmas story. Did you see the story unfold in a children's pageant at church? Did you sit in the lap of a parent or a grandparent, reading together from a children's Bible storybook? Did you talk about the events surrounding Jesus' birth as your little fingers positioned and repositioned the figures in a ceramic Nativity scene?

Perhaps as a youth you were a player in an outdoor live Nativity scene. Perhaps you listened as the Christmas story was read aloud from one of the Gospels during a worship service. Try to recall the plot line and all the characters involved. Chances are that the Christmas story etched in your memory is a composite of the accounts in Matthew and Luke, probably with embellishments and omissions.

The Gospel of Matthew tells the story of Jesus' birth and the events surrounding it in a particular way. It begins by tracing family lineage but with a different list of names than in Luke. The writer of Matthew reminds the reader of Old Testament passages that he now recognizes as prophesies of Jesus.

In Matthew's Gospel an angel appears—not to Mary but to Joseph. There is a wondrous star in the sky instead of a choir of angels. Wise men, not shepherds, come to honor Jesus. There is no mention of the Roman Empire, instead, a shrewd and brutal King Herod. Why do you suppose Matthew tells the Christmas story this way? What does the Gospel writer want you to notice?

Enter the Bible Story

Emile Cailliet, for many years a distinguished professor of philosophy at Princeton Theological Seminary, never saw a Bible until he was twenty-three years old. By that time he had already served in the French army in World War I and was beginning to establish himself as one of France's brightest young scholars. When the Bible came to his hands, he opened it—quite by chance—to the Beatitudes in the Gospel of Matthew. As he read, he realized, with "awe and wonder," that this was the book that understood him. This was the book that in all of his studies he had unknowingly been seeking.[1]

That word would please the author of Matthew's Gospel and all of those first-century readers who not only read and memorized its pages but who made handwritten copies for other readers. For some readers then and now, Matthew is their introduction to Jesus of Nazareth, the Christ of God. For others who already believe, Matthew answers many of their questions about Jesus: his birth, his teachings, his death and resurrection. Especially, Matthew introduces us to Jesus' teachings about the kingdom of heaven, teachings that raise questions even as they give answers and demands.

Above all, however, as you look at Matthew thoughtfully and—better yet, reverently—you see it is a book that knows you and that challenges you to a new, more wonderful, more demanding life.

Matthew and the Hebrew Scriptures

Most Bible scholars feel that Mark was the first Gospel written. Why then is Matthew the opening book in our New Testament? Quite clearly, because this Gospel makes the most direct tie with the Hebrew Scriptures, thus indicating that the two testaments belong together, that the best basis for understanding the New Testament is found in the Hebrew Scriptures, and that we call these Scriptures the "Old" Testament because they precede the New Testament and prepare us for understanding it.

A thoughtful reader might easily think that Matthew's primary aim is to show this connection. He begins in a "Hebrew" way: "A record of the ancestors of Jesus Christ, son of David, son of Abraham" (Matthew 1:1). The Hebrew Scriptures are full of genealogies, as we discover especially in

Genesis, Ruth, Chronicles, Ezra, and Nehemiah. The Hebrew Scriptures also emphasize history, because their writers believed that God is at work in history. Thus Matthew summarizes his genealogy by historical periods: "So there were fourteen generations from Abraham to David, fourteen generations from David to the exile to Babylon, and fourteen generations from the exile to Babylon to the Christ" (1:17).

An earnest first-century Jew would see the history of his or her people as breaking naturally into a period from Abraham, the father of their nation, to David, their epochal king. Then the period continues with David to the Babylonian captivity, the crisis that most severely tested their nationhood and that at the same time sealed their identity as the people of the Scriptures and the synagogue as the place of learning.

Matthew adds what he sees as the third great period, from Babylon "to the Christ." He presents Jesus Christ as the ultimate fact of his people's history. All else is prelude.

See, then, who Jesus Christ is. On the one hand, he is the product of a long line of Jewish generations and a figure in history like any other human figure. At the same time, he is the breaking point in history, God's unique invasion into our human story. Mind you, as I indicated a moment ago, the Jews believed that God was always operating in history. This event, the birth of Jesus Christ, however, was an event like no other *in* history and yet *beyond* history.

Matthew makes still another tie to the Hebrew Scriptures when he reports on the unique circumstances of Jesus' conception: "Now all of this took place so that what the Lord had spoken through the prophet would be fulfilled" (1:22). The Hebrew writers are quoted throughout the New Testament; but this phrase, "spoken through the prophet," is a favorite with Matthew. By it he reaffirms the connection between the Hebrew Scriptures and what he himself is writing. For Matthew it is a seamless unit.

In its own way, Matthew is a scandalous book. The genealogy follows the usual Hebrew pattern of identifying children through the line of the father. Unlike most such genealogies, however, this one introduces the mother on four occasions: Tamar (1:3), Rahab (1:5), Ruth (1:5), and "the wife of Uriah" (1:6).

Matthew and the Hebrew Scriptures

Citation in Matthew	Old Testament Reference
Matthew 1:21, 23 Mary's son is named "Jesus, because he will save his people from their sins."	*Jesus* is the Greek form of the Hebrew name *Joshua*, which means "God helps" or "God saves."
Matthew 1:23 Matthew quotes the Greek (Septuagint) version of Isaiah 7:14.	*Isaiah 7:14* Promise of a son, to be named Immanuel
Matthew 2:6 Herod's advisors cite Micah 5:2 to identify where the Messiah will be born.	*Micah 5:2* Prophecy of a ruler of Israel that will come from Bethlehem
Matthew 2:15 "I have called my son out of Egypt."	*Exodus 1–15* God's deliverance of Israel from slavery in Egypt *Hosea 11:1* "When Israel was a child, I loved him, / and out of Egypt I called my son" (NRSV).
Matthew 2:16 King Herod orders the massacre of infant boys in Bethlehem.	*Exodus 1:15-22* Pharaoh orders the death of Hebrew boys.
Matthew 2:18 In connection with Herod's slaughter of the infants, Matthew cites Jeremiah 31:15.	*Jeremiah 31:15* "Rachel is weeping for her children" (NRSV).
Matthew 2:23 "He will be called a Nazarene."	The exact words do not appear in the Old Testament. Matthew may intend an allusion to "nazirite," a person set apart as holy (Numbers 6; Judges 13:5, 7).

If you know the Hebrew Scriptures as did the first Christians, you would know that (1) Tamar's twins were born of an incestuous union with her father-in-law; (2) Rahab had been a prostitute in Jericho; (3) Ruth was a woman of Moab, a nation with whom Jews were not supposed to intermarry; (4) and "the wife of Uriah"—well, her name was Bathsheba; but when Matthew identifies her not by her name but by her being "the wife of Uriah," he is reminding his readers that she and King David first came to know one another in an adulterous relationship. Matthew's use of the phrase that ties her to her first husband is a sharp, stark reminder of David and Bathsheba's history, an element so significant that even the eventual product of their union, Solomon, is not enough to justify their past.

However, it isn't quite right to speak of Matthew as a "scandalous" book. Rather, it is a typical biblical book in that it portrays the human story as it is, the story of human beings, with our strange mix of the base and the noble, the sinner and the saint, the misery and the grandeur that characterizes all humans. The Bible isn't always a pretty book, but it is always an honest book. It never uses evil to titillate, as do some contemporary novels and sitcoms. It never denies that evil exists, and it doesn't carefully skirt around troublesome data.

Still more important, the Bible in general and Chapter 1 of Matthew in particular make clear that God isn't discouraged by our human sinfulness. God sends the Redeemer through a genealogical line that has its fair share of people we'd rather omit from our ancestral record, as if to make clear that while sin is not good, neither is it victorious: God can work in the midst of its mess.

Perhaps one of the overlooked factors in Mary's being a virgin is to say rather dramatically that God breaks into the all-too-typical line of sin with the classical symbol of purity: a virgin. It is as if the virgin's appearance overcomes all that has come before. Sin may mark our human story; but victorious divine intervention is our story's ceaseless, sometimes unbelievable, wonder.

Matthew Tells the Story

Matthew finishes his genealogy and then continues almost matter-of-factly: "This is how the birth of Jesus Christ took place" (1:18). We're hardly ready for the story that follows: a typical village couple, Joseph and Mary (the girl in her early teens), in the year of their engagement. In their culture, the year of engagement or betrothal was one in which they were considered legally married, except for the right of cohabiting. If the man were to die within that year, the woman was legally identified as a widow, even though still a virgin. At this point, as Matthew reports it, the young woman, Mary, "became pregnant by the Holy Spirit" (1:18).

Joseph's first response is, by the law of his time and culture, generous. He wanted to avoid public humiliation for Mary and began arranging for a quiet dissolution of their engagement. However, an angel intervened in a dream, telling him not to be afraid because Mary's child was from the Holy Spirit. Then Joseph was given a significant bonus: The name of the child was revealed to him; and he was to give the name *Jesus*, "because he will save his people from their sins" (1:21).

As Matthew continues the story, he reminds his readers of another name for this child: *Emmanuel*, meaning "God with us." Jesus of Nazareth was to be God's singular visitor to planet Earth. Matthew then adds an earthy but significant detail: that Joseph "didn't have sexual relations with her until she gave birth to a son" (1:25), thus underlining the quality of Mary's virginity.

At this point the story takes a dramatic, romantic turn—the coming of the wise men. This is Matthew's way of indicating that though Jesus comes from the line of David and the kings of Israel, he is a worldwide figure. As I see it, the wise men are not only representatives of another ethnic culture but are also a bridge between the Hebrew prophets and the wisdom of the Gentile world.

The wise men made their journey by light of their best scholarly studies of the stars and probably of their philosophical writers. However, they received their final direction by way of rabbis who pointed to the writing

The Magi in Matthew

These mysterious Gentile visitors "from the east" (meaning Babylon, Persia, or the Arabian Peninsula) were not kings but wealthy astrologers, probably members of a priestly class. As scholars steeped in Zoroastrian theology and tradition, they were expecting a savior who would come to establish a kingdom of righteousness. The Gospel of Matthew regards their visit as an affirmation of the universal claim and international recognition of Jesus as the expected King.

of the Hebrew prophet Micah, who had identified Bethlehem as the birthplace of Israel's coming king.

History seems to indicate that there are times of particular spiritual hunger, when people are more sensitive to the Spirit of God. Certainly this was true of the period in which Jesus Christ was born. Greeks, Romans, and Jews alike were on the quest. The Greeks were in search of better forms of government; the Romans, in their aggressive way, were establishing enforced world peace; and the Jews had a new hunger for freedom and for their promised Messiah.

Now East and West meet via the Hebrew prophets and the best knowledge of the Gentile scholars. The prophet Micah, via Herod's counselors, completed the journey for the star-led wise men, so they could lay their offerings at the feet of the Baby born to peasants from the hill country town of Nazareth.

The Story's First Villain

However, no story on our planet goes far before a villain appears. Joseph could have been such a villain, a well-meaning one, simply seeking to protect his own justified rights; but Joseph was a good and righteous man. He was restrained from thwarting the purposes of God. I'm quite sure there's something for all of us to learn in Joseph's story. Often God's best purposes are delayed or temporarily frustrated by those of us whose intentions are right but whose vision is narrow. Fortunately, Joseph was receptive enough before God to become an aide to the divine plan rather than a deterrent.

Not so with King Herod. Where Joseph was a good and righteous man, Herod was a fearful and conflicted one. In many ways, Herod had been an especially good and generous king to the Jews; but he was a man maniacally suspicious of everyone, fearful someone would take his throne from him. Driven by that fear, over the years Herod ordered the death of his wife, his mother-in-law, his oldest son, and two other of his sons in a psychotic drive to protect his throne. So when wise men appeared in Jerusalem looking for the new King of the Jews, it's easy to predict how Herod would respond.

Herod may have been mad, but he was no fool. He inquired of his religious and legal experts (the two were often one in first-century Judaism, since the law of Israel was the law of the Scriptures) to learn where the Messiah was to be born. They directed Herod's attention to the prophecies of Micah (Micah 5:2) that identified Bethlehem.

Then Herod secretly called for the wise men to learn when they had first begun following the star and also, of course, to win their loyalty by assisting them with the information about Bethlehem. "Go and search carefully for the child," Herod said. "When you've found him, report to me so that I too may go and honor him" (Matthew 2:8). Herod's honor to potential kings had a deadly quality!

So, ironically, with Herod's assistance, the magi made their way to Bethlehem. If there was a miracle in the wise men's search and in the human assistance of the counselors in the king's court who narrowed their search, the greatest miracle was in the magi's recognition of the Baby being cared for by the teenage peasant girl and her carpenter husband. The wise men knew how a king should look and the accoutrements that should mark his setting. None of these expectations were fulfilled in this Child. To see a king in such ordinariness required a leap of faith.

The magi made such a leap. In fact, they made that leap with such certainty that they not only presented their expensive gifts, but they chose to return home by another route in order to avoid the promised meeting with King Herod. The twentieth century's premier poet T. S. Eliot, who knew something himself about a leap of faith in his conversion to Christianity, described what happened to the wise men as seeing "a Birth, certainly," but also for them a "Death, our death," because they could no longer be at ease with their old gods.[2] The challenge of the Christ, whether in his birth, his death, and resurrection, is to receive him as Lord of life and to give up our old lives in order to become his disciples.

At this point the Christmas story takes a bitter turn, something in harsh contrast to the mood of our conventional Christmas cards. Frustrated by the realization that the wise men had fooled him, Herod visited upon the Bethlehem area the same insane murderous tactic that had meant the decimation of his royal family. He ordered the execution of all male children in the area two years old and younger.

The actual number of deaths would not have been large, since it was an area of small population; but the ruthless act and its incongruity with the birth of our Lord is a grotesque dramatization of the unceasing war between good and evil and the innocent victims of this eternal struggle. It reminds us again that the Bible is never simply a feel-good book but an honest one— sometimes more honest than the earnest, sentimental reader wants to hear.

The Trip to Egypt

Joseph had already been warned in a dream and had escaped with Mary and the Infant to Egypt. Tradition says that they remained in Egypt perhaps two years, long enough that Egypt's Coptic Christians have several sites and legends about the time the Holy Family spent there.

In time, Joseph was again counseled in a dream. He was told that Herod was dead and that the family should settle in Galilee where there was more security. They made their home in Nazareth, so it is that our Lord is known as Jesus of Nazareth.

Nazareth was a city on the edge of one of the great caravan roads of the ancient world, where traders traveling between Damascus and Egypt could be seen daily. Still, the city was a strangely sheltered place in the hills where the people had an accent of their own and lives that generally were free of the influences of Rome and Athens. Here Jesus the Nazarene was to prepare for the three years that would change the history of our human race.

Live the Story

What would you be missing if you didn't know the Christmas story as Matthew tells it? Oddly enough, some Christians are startled to learn that Jesus was a Jew. Matthew rehearses Jesus' roots in the history of Israel and in the Hebrew Scriptures to make clear that Jesus is the fulfillment, not the repudiation, of that heritage. Think about the particular names in the genealogy, women as well as men. What does that suggest about the way God works? What does it suggest about how God might use a person like you?

What would you be missing if you didn't know about Joseph's special role in the story? Imagine how he must have felt! Consider the difference —for Joseph and for you—between doing the conventionally proper thing and trusting God to bring about something new in a difficult situation.

What would you be missing if Matthew hadn't mentioned the magi, learned visitors from a land far beyond Israel's borders? God seems to be at work among the wise as well as the simple, from every background, wherever minds are searching and hearts are open. You may never see a celestial miracle, but God may still be calling you.

What would you be missing if Matthew hadn't told you about the murderous rage of Herod? If all you knew was the happy, domesticated story told by Christmas greeting cards, you might wonder what that has to do with your world where violence happens daily. The Gospel of Matthew recognizes that evil was terrible then as it is now but not ultimately able to thwart God's purposes.

Spend a few minutes dwelling with Matthew's account of the coming of Jesus. Close your eyes and imagine yourself in the midst of it all. Ask God to speak to you through this marvelous and mysterious story.

[1] From *Eternity Magazine* (July 1974).
[2] From "Journey of the Magi" in *The Waste Land and Other Poems*, by T. S. Eliot (Harcourt, Brace and World, Inc., 1934); page 70.

2.

Jesus' Identity Is Confirmed and Tested

Matthew 3–4

Claim Your Story

Do you remember your baptism? If you were baptized as an infant or a toddler, you probably have to rely on family documentation such as a baptismal certificate; a small New Testament with your name and a date written on the flyleaf; or a photo of you wearing a fancy gown, surrounded by parents, grandparents, aunts and uncles, or perhaps godparents.

If you were baptized when you were older, you probably can recall some of what happened. Perhaps you were dressed in your Sunday best and felt a sprinkling of water on your head. Maybe your head and shoulders were doused with a pitcher of water, the runoff soaking into your clothes. Maybe you were plunged underwater in the chilly water of a river, a lake, or the ocean surf.

Whatever the logistics were at the time, what does your baptism mean to you now? To whom or to what does it connect you?

In contrast to your memory of your baptism, your memories of facing temptations are undoubtedly clear, even vivid and perhaps troubling, depending on how you responded. Have you ever wondered, looking back on those decisions, why you did what you did? You may have wanted something badly and didn't think it would come your way without taking matters into your own hands.

At one level, you believe that God has your best interests at heart, that God wants you to enjoy abundant life. However, living that conviction requires trusting that you are one of God's children. That issue of trust underlies the three basic tests that Israel faced, that Jesus faced in the wilderness following his baptism, and that we as members of the church continue to face.

Enter the Bible Story

Every age has its prophets, though we don't call them that. In our times, we call them political pundits, economic forecasters, or guest experts for our news networks. Ancient Israel had a more demanding expectation: They wanted a person who could deliver a message from God. They had been without a bona fide prophet for three or four centuries by the time John the Baptist appeared on the scene. I think that John, bigger-than-life, made up for the hiatus.

Matthew introduces John to us almost the way the Old Testament writer introduced the prophet Elijah, with no preliminary data, as if the person had credentials enough in himself, without any supplementary data (compare 1 Kings 17:1 and Matthew 3:1).

John "appeared" in an unlikely place, "the desert of Judea," unlikely in that John had a message to deliver to his entire nation, and a desert wasn't a place to find a crowd. Indeed, one has to wonder how people first got to know about John. When Ralph Waldo Emerson is believed to have said that if a man preaches a better sermon, "tho' he build his house in the woods, the world will make a beaten path to his door,"[1] he could well have had John the Baptist in the back of his mind, because John's setting was anything but inviting.

Nor did John cater to his audience. His was no prosperity gospel, no comforting word. He wore clothes made of camel's hair and a leather belt and lived on a diet of locusts and wild honey, and his message fit his wardrobe and menu. "Change your hearts and lives!" he cried, "Here comes the kingdom of heaven!" (3:2). I appreciate this wording in the Common English Bible (CEB). We're accustomed to the word *repent* in other translations, which is a grand theological word but one lost to us by its familiarity and perhaps by its religiosity. We too easily think of repentance as feelings of regret, while in truth it means a dramatic change in life and conduct.

About the Scripture

The Kingdom of Heaven

Contrary to some popular assumptions, the *kingdom of heaven* does not refer to an otherworldly, future reality. Rather, it is equivalent to the *kingdom of God* in the other Synoptic Gospels, meaning the reign of God or the rule of God. The Gospel of Matthew prefers the term *kingdom of heaven* in accordance with a Jewish custom that, as a sign of reverence, avoided writing or speaking aloud the name of God.

Why was John calling for such a change? Because "here comes the kingdom of heaven!" That phrase sounds like a warning, and in a sense it is. However, it is the warning of opportunity. The kingdom of heaven is God's grand purpose and plan for our world, so to be ready for it is to be blessed beyond measure; but to miss it is disaster.

Great numbers of those who heard John got the point. They confessed their sins—the crucial first step to a change of life—and submitted to John's baptism in the Jordan River. Eventually the movers and shakers of first-century Jewish life, the Pharisees and Sadducees, came for baptism, too. I honor them for this. Perhaps some of them were pandering to the crowds, wanting to win their favor by playing on the popularity of John; but I suspect that many were sincere in hungering for a deeper faith.

Despite their willingness to be baptized, John called them "children of snakes" and told them to produce evidence that they were ready to change. Then, still more incisively, he told them that their good family name ("Abraham is our father") wouldn't cut it for them; God could find better followers from the stones of the field. I wonder how John the Baptist would fare today in a national denominational meeting or an address to the joint houses of Congress or, for that matter, in any typical local church.

However, John indicated that he had nothing to lose. He was not trying to build a personal following, he explained. He was simply preparing the way for another, for someone whose sandals he was unworthy to carry, so what the crowds thought of him mattered not a whit.

The Baptism of Jesus

Then one day, he came. Jesus came from Galilee to the Jordan, seeking baptism from John. John, who had so easily brushed off members of the Jerusalem power structure, now fumbled an apology to a carpenter from Nazareth: "I need to be baptized by you, yet you come to me?" Jesus answered, "This is necessary to fulfill all righteousness" (3:14-15).

Jesus' answer is a guideline for any number of questions that face individual believers and Christian institutions. Jesus refused to consider himself above the structures of the faith community. He submitted to the same gates of entry, the same routine exercised as the vast variety of souls who were seeking baptism from John at the Jordan River. By his act Jesus gave added significance to the wonderful democracy of true faith: No one is so bad as to be shut out, and no one is so good as to be granted special privileges. It isn't enough to be "spiritual"; we need also to submit ourselves to the disciplines of religious practice.

As Jesus emerged from the rite of baptism, he received recognition from heaven As he came from the water, Jesus saw the Spirit of God coming to him "like a dove and resting on him" and then a voice hailing him as God's Son, the source of God's pleasure. Matthew doesn't tell us if John or any of the bystanders saw or heard this divine visitation. Perhaps it was for Jesus alone. Some of God's gracious visitations in our lives are meant to be shared with others to the benefit of their faith-walk; but some are intimate, wonderfully crucial to our experiences but best hidden within our own hearts.

About the Christian Faith

Hints of the Trinity

The doctrine of the Trinity was fully developed only after New Testament times. However, the Trinitarian baptismal formula does appear in Matthew 28:19 ("in the name of the Father and of the Son and of the Holy Spirit"). While it would be a mistake to read Matthew 3:13-17 as a full exposition of the doctrine of the Trinity, the story of Jesus' baptism does present all three persons of the Trinity—Father, Son, and Spirit—in relationship.

Baptism, whatever its form or whenever it happens, is never simply an end in itself. It was not for Jesus, nor is it for us. In Jesus' case, the baptism and the divine visit that accompanied it seem to have been preparation for a crisis, perhaps the greatest crisis in Jesus' life until Gethsemane and Calvary. Jesus went, under the Spirit's direction, to a place alone. This place was a wilderness/desert place where he could complete the transition from Nazareth carpenter to teacher, preacher, healer, and redeemer.

The Temptation in the Wilderness

I feel obliged to walk softly as we follow Jesus into this wilderness. I wonder what our Lord expected as he entered this journey. He knew it would be lonely; the setting guaranteed that. He knew, too, that he would endure a soul-wrenching experience; one has no business turning to God without expecting God to be God. That is, God is the source, we are the seekers, and therefore God can name the price for the favors we ask.

I suspect that the fallacy in much of popular religion—the kind that shows itself in calling upon God only in times of need—is that such religion sees God as powerful enough to grant the help we need yet not so powerful as to make demands on us.

In Jesus' forty days in the wilderness, the temptations were from Satan, but the demands were from God. The flip side of every temptation is God's expectation. Is the temptation toward greed? God's expectation is generosity. Is the temptation to lust? God expects purity. Are we tempted to mediocrity? God expects—yes, demands—excellence.

When Jesus chose to fast and pray for forty days, the number was not chosen casually. Forty is a symbolic number in the Scriptures, emphasizing judgment or testing. Thus the flood waters came for forty days (Genesis 7:12); Israel's spies researched the Promised Land for forty days (Numbers 13:25); and the nation was compelled to remain in the wilderness for forty years following their unfaithfulness (Numbers 14:34). Jesus sought God for forty days and thus submitted himself to testing for that time.

The climax of the testing came at the end of the period. Hunger asserted itself. "He was starving," as the CEB translation puts it. The need

About the Christian Faith

Jesus as Truly Human

Docetism is a doctrine that was popular in the early church but eventually was rejected by the church as heretical. This belief claimed that Jesus didn't have a real physical body but only the appearance of a body. Docetism was often combined with a dualistic view that only the purely spiritual can be good while matter is evil. The Gospel of Matthew implicitly challenges docetism by portraying Jesus as a helpless infant and one who will later suffer and die. The Apostles' Creed guarded against docetism by affirming that Jesus "was born of the Virgin Mary, suffered under Pontius Pilate, and was crucified, dead, and buried." So the Gospel and the Creed testify that Jesus was truly human.

provided an avenue for temptation. I suspect that every temptation enters our lives by some avenue of need. What complicates our lives is that these needs are likely to be legitimate ones. Jesus had a right to be hungry; hunger is the first demand an infant asserts upon coming into this world. Why shouldn't Jesus be hungry, and why shouldn't he get satisfaction?

So, too, we humans hunger for affection. Why shouldn't we satisfy that hunger regardless of the bonds of commitment? We hunger for recognition. Why shouldn't we get it, even if we have to deceive or disparage others in order to achieve it? We are hungry creatures; and there's likely to be a voice that tells us, "You're entitled! You have your rights."

The tempter made the argument of entitlement especially powerful in Jesus' case. "Since you are God's Son, command these stones to become bread" (Matthew 4:3). It's interesting that the tempter spoke back to Jesus the message Jesus heard at his baptism: "My Son whom I love." Temptation is never as enticing and convincing as when it puts on a spiritual face.

I often ponder the wisdom of Blaise Pascal, the mathematical and scientific genius who was also a passionate believer: "Men never do evil so completely and cheerfully as when they do it from religious conviction."[2] If the tempter can cloak temptation in a sacred garment, it will confuse even the devout. Jesus countered with Scripture: "One does not live by bread alone, but by every word that comes from the mouth of the LORD" (Deuteronomy 8:3).

The second temptation had to do with Jesus' identity. Placing him on the high point of the Temple, the tempter chided, "Since you are God's Son, throw yourself down; for it is written, I will command my angels concerning you, and they will take you up in their hands so that you won't hit your foot on a stone." Now the temptation was fortified by Scripture itself. What further argument was necessary?

I think there's something for us to learn here that we should note in passing. All Scripture should be read within its own context rather than as an excerpt like movie endorsements. Further, each Scripture should be read within the context of the whole body of Scripture. If we believe that all Scripture is from God, then we shouldn't use a single passage without recognizing its place in the larger body from which we've taken it. Jesus followed this latter rule, balancing the tempting quotation from Psalm 91:11-12 by a quotation from Deuteronomy 6:16.

The third temptation came in a direct offer from the tempter. In a sense, it is nothing other than an adaptation of the temptation in the garden of Eden, the oldest of all temptations. In Eden the tempter urged Adam and Eve to take of the forbidden fruit so they could be like God. It was a foolish offer because they were already made in God's image and possessed by that right all the godliness appropriate to their human role. Genesis tells us that they gave up by their sin.

The tempter urged Jesus to bow down and worship him, for which the tempter promised him "all the kingdoms of the world and their glory." Again Jesus replied with Scripture and ordered Satan to leave him.

A further word should be said about this third temptation. Let me call it the temptation of shortcuts. The road of God's will is not only straight and narrow, but it is also frustratingly unhurried. We want our successes, our fulfillments, and our sense of purpose without delay. We need instead to learn respect for "God's good time."

The Book of Revelation describes a time when the kingdom of the world will become the kingdom of our Lord and of his Christ (Revelation 11:15). The tempter was offering a shortcut, just as the tempter does for all of us, day after day. Jesus knew what you and I must remember: The tempter cannot deliver on his promises, so the shortcut is a dead end.

Across the Testaments

Matthew and the Hebrew Scriptures

Citation in Matthew	Old Testament Reference
Matthew 3:3 "This is the one of whom the prophet Isaiah spoke when he said, 'The voice of one crying in the wilderness' " (New Revised Standard Version).	*Isaiah 40:3* "A voice cries out: 'In the wilderness prepare the way of the LORD' " (NRSV).
Matthew 3:4 John the Baptist's clothing	*2 Kings 1:8* Description of Elijah
Matthew 3:9 "Abraham is our father."	*Genesis 17:1-7* Covenant with Abraham
Matthew 4:2 Jesus fasts 40 days.	*Exodus 34:28* Moses fasts 40 days.
Matthew 4:4 Jesus quotes Deuteronomy 8:3.	*Deuteronomy 8:3* "One does not live by bread alone (NRSV).
Matthew 4:5-6 The devil cites Psalm 91:11-12.	*Psalm 91:11-12* Angels will protect you from harm.
Matthew 4:7 Jesus quotes Deuteronomy 6:16.	Deuteronomy 6:16 "Do not put the Lord your God to the test (NRSV).
Matthew 4:10 Worship and serve God only.	*Deuteronomy 6:13* Worship and serve God only.
Matthew 4:13 Territory Matthew associates with Gentiles	*Joshua 19:10-16, 32-39* Land is allocated to two Israelite tribes.
Matthew 4:16 Quotations of Isaiah 9:1-2	*Isaiah 9:1-2* Light dispels the darkness.

The Overarching Temptation

Before we leave this scene, we should note one more issue. All of the temptations presented to Jesus had to do with the use of power. We never know what we're made of until power is placed in our hands. This is true whether it is as large as the power of a presidency or as commonplace as the power of a driver's license. Lord Acton, the British historian, warned, "Power tends to corrupt, and absolute power corrupts absolutely."[3] The Scriptures taught it before Lord Acton said it. What's worse, the illusion of power is as deceptive as power itself.

The wilderness experience ends with a lovely word. When Jesus rejected the last of the temptations, "the devil left him, and angels came and took care of him" (Matthew 4:11). We open the door for heavenly visits when we close the door to temptation.

Capernaum and Choosing Disciples

After spending most of his life in Nazareth, Jesus moved on to Capernaum. Hereafter this is referred to as his home. There he began preaching. His message was the same as that of John the Baptist, a call for a change of heart because the kingdom of heaven is near.

We will see the term *the kingdom of heaven* or *the kingdom of God* throughout the Gospels of Matthew, Mark, and Luke. One wonders why it is no longer a dominant part of our thinking and living. I suspect that our culture unconsciously prefers the image of an elected Lord, so to speak, rather than a king.

At this point Matthew announces a strategic change in Jesus' ministry as he called disciples to join him, including two pairs of fishermen-brothers—Simon (Peter) and Andrew, and James and John. Jesus approached them at their places of work. In the case of Simon and Andrew, he appealed to them in the language of their current labor: "Come, follow me, and I'll show you how to fish for people" (4:19).

On what basis did Jesus choose these team members? Only a few stand out; and one of the more noticeable ones, Judas Iscariot, proved to be a traitor. Yet it is on these relatively routine figures that Jesus built his church.

Soon Jesus became a traveling teacher, going throughout Galilee, teaching in synagogues (4:23). His theme was still the Kingdom, but Matthew notes that it was "the good news [gospel]" of the Kingdom. Jesus delivered this good news not only in the message of his teaching and preaching but also in the demonstration of his message, healing "every disease and sickness among the people." Naturally, news of such wonders began to spread; Matthew notes particularly that the word reached Syria. People began to bring their sick to him. Matthew lists some of the cases ranging simply from "pain" to epilepsy, paralysis, and those "possessed by demons."

We need not be condescending or unduly spiritual about the phrase *possessed by demons*. At the least it describes those illnesses for which we have no explanation. It's interesting that in our present generation, when our great research centers find new answers every day, we still find ourselves baffled by so much of the intricate mechanism of the human body and mind. At the most, we should know that there is in our world the monstrous fact of evil, of which we know little and which challenges us in so many forms.

Live the Story

John the Baptist insisted on repentance and a new start. The crowds heard him, and many were convinced. I'm sure many others walked away, disappointed and uncomfortable. Does John's call for a change of heart or a new way of living resonate with you? What might that entail?

It's interesting that Jesus, whose spirituality was so evident that John was reluctant to baptize him, insisted that he must accept the role of religious ritual, a vigorous challenge to our age of independent spirituality. How do church rituals help you connect with God and the community of believers?

Tests of one kind and another come into every person's life. Some are almost routine, but some are life-shaking. For Jesus, it was a wilderness. For some of us, it is a broken relationship, a job loss, a life-threatening illness, or a failure of heartbreaking proportions. What temptations have you encountered? How did those experiences affect your relationship with God? I dare to feel that we can expect God's angels to minister to us at such times.

As Jesus called Simon, Andrew, James, and John to follow him, we acknowledge that he is calling us, too. Twenty centuries of persons like you and me, in every part of the world, have recognized that the ranks of the disciples were not completed by the first twelve. Every new generation and every new community call for new followers.

What are you being called to do? Who are you being called to be? Meditate for a few minutes on the direction you believe God is calling you to take. Meditate for a few minutes on the direction you believe God is calling you to take.

---

[1]From *www.transcendalists.com/emerson_quotes.htm*.
[2]From *brainyquote.com/quotes/authors/b/blaise_pascal_4.html*.
[3]From *bartleby.com*.

3.

The Sermon on the Mount

Matthew 5–7

Claim Your Story

Remember for a moment a time when you took your small child, a grand-child, or perhaps a neighbor's child to McDonald's. Chances are that you heard and acquiesced to a plea for a Happy Meal. What was so special about that meal? The prize, of course! Did it bring happiness? Perhaps it brought a few minutes of excitement, but the "happy" probably wore off quickly, leaving only the desire for return trips to McDonald's for more Happy Meals.

When we get older, we don't necessarily get wiser; the prizes we seek just get more expensive. Make a mental list of the advertisements you saw this past week on TV, the Internet, magazines, or billboards. What products were thrust before your eyes? Expensive cars? fashionable clothes? rich food and drink? fabulous vacations? romantic relationships? Which of those would help make you happy?

In the Beatitudes, Jesus speaks about what it means to be deeply happy, deeply joyful, deeply blessed. However, the Beatitudes—and in fact most of Jesus' Sermon on the Mount—completely reverse the values of most societies, including ours. Is that reversal something that you welcome, or does it make you uncomfortable? What would it take to make you gen-uinely happy, joyful, blessed?

Enter the Bible Story

Reported in the Gospel of Matthew is a sermon that Jesus preached that has blessed, challenged, and troubled humanity ever since. Matthew sets the physical scene before reporting this sermon and then concludes the report by another reference to the setting, but the two reports seem somewhat contradictory. At the outset we're told that when Jesus saw the crowds gathering he went up the mountain and sat down. Then the disciples came to him, which suggests that Jesus was talking only to his disciples. However, at the sermon's conclusion we read, "When Jesus finished these words, the crowds were amazed at his teaching because he was teaching them like someone with authority and not like their legal experts" (7:28), which indicates that the crowd heard it all.

Personally, I think that Jesus brought his disciples up close so that he could make them his primary audience. However, the crowds pressed in as near as possible in order to take full advantage of Jesus' teaching. They were fully taken by what Jesus said. Indeed, I'm sure some of the listening fringe eventually became faithful followers. If so, they must have been thorough converts. If having heard the wonders and the strenuous claims of Kingdom life they were still persuaded to buy into the Kingdom, then they must surely have been profoundly changed.

Whether the audience was primarily the disciples or the more conglomerate crowd surrounding them, remember that this initial audience was what would have been known in that day as the people of the earth, common people who by their limited education or by the demands of hard daily toil had little time for study and therefore were generally seen as poor prospects for religious leadership. Yet these people—not the scribes and Pharisees, the professionally religious—were the ones who first heard the call to the new life of the Kingdom.

Jesus underlined that his Kingdom is to be lived out in this world. It is not to be discussed to death in learned assemblies nor pursued in holy isolation, but the Kingdom life is to be walked and practiced in the field and the marketplace.

The Beatific Life

The sermon begins with what we call the Beatitudes, the words of blessing. The dictionary defines *beatitude* as "supreme blessedness, exalted happiness." In these Beatitudes, Jesus gives *happiness* a new definition. He

Matthew and the Hebrew Scriptures

Citation in Matthew	Old Testament Reference
Matthew 5:1 Jesus goes up the mountain.	*Exodus 19* Moses receives the Law of Mount Sinai.
Matthew 5:21 Do not be angry.	*Exodus 20:13* Do not murder.
Matthew 5:27 Do not lust.	*Exodus 20:14* Do not commit adultery.
Matthew 5:31-32 Jesus challenges men's unlimited right to divorce.	*Deuteronomy 24:1-4* The Law addresses divorce.
Matthew 5:33-37 Do not make oaths.	*Exodus 20:7* Do not make wrongful use of the Lord's name. *Leviticus 19:12* Do not swear falsely.
Matthew 5:38-42 Do not respond to violence with violence.	*Exodus 21:24* Revenge should be proportionate to the offence.
Matthew 5:43-48 Love even your enemies.	*Leviticus 19:18* Love your neighbor as yourself.

includes within its boundaries experiences such as mourning and persecution, elements that ordinarily seem the opposite of happiness. In other words, Jesus promises happiness of such power that it takes over territory that is customarily seen as cursed.

So it is throughout this remarkable body of teaching. The laws and conduct that we make manageable by our narrow definitions, Jesus makes challenging by broadening their application. The daily issues that drive us to worry become quite trivial in Jesus' teaching. The excuses with which we justify our conduct embarrass us by their shallowness.

Let's examine the particulars of the sermon. Following the Beatitudes, Jesus told his followers (including us) their assignment. We are to be salt in a culture that tends to self-corruption. We are to be light in a world that lives in darkness and seems often to seek it—sometimes because we want to hide our unacceptable deeds and sometimes because we hardly know our way to the light.

Salt and light are powerful out of all proportion to their size. A little salt seasons a large amount and preserves that which would otherwise decay. A single candle pierces a room consumed by darkness. I don't mean to build a doctrine around a metaphor; but perhaps when Jesus tells us that we are salt and light, it is a kind of rebuke to our excitement about our size and prominence. As Christ's followers we are to be notable not for our quantity but for our quality.

Perhaps the greatest failure of the church is not our poor evangelism but our even poorer discipleship. Indeed, if the church were more demonstrably different from our daily culture, perhaps much of our evangelism would happen through the attractiveness people would find in our lives.

The next section of Jesus' teaching (5:17-20) prepared his listeners for what was to follow. He promised that he had not come to "do away with the Law and the Prophets" but rather "to fulfill them." We're inclined to cut the Law and the prophets to fit our size and inclinations. Even the earnest, quite passionate Pharisees did so.

I suspect that the people in Jesus' immediate audience were startled when Jesus told them that their righteousness would have to be greater than that of the Pharisees and the professional students of the Law. It would be as if someone were to tell a contemporary congregation, "You'll never make it unless you're better Christians than your preachers, priests, and seminary professors." Of course the people of Jesus' day were much more conscious of cultural, intellectual, and economic barriers than we are today, so Jesus' words shocked them all the more.

Inward Thought and Outward Conduct

Jesus then proceeded to extend Moses' laws regarding murder and adultery to the inward life. How far we are still from understanding Jesus' teachings or from taking them seriously!

A number of years ago, when a presidential candidate confessed that he had committed adultery in his heart, the secular press was quite amused, the point being that everyone entertains such thoughts, so why should one be concerned about it? So, too, with Jesus' warning against anger and harsh words. We want to answer, "But everyone has lustful thoughts, or calls someone stupid," and Jesus answers quietly, "But you shouldn't." Suddenly the Law and the prophets become bigger than we realized.

How do we handle the new law of Christ: Turn the other cheek, go the extra mile, give to the poor. I have trouble with these commands because I ask myself what it does to the other party: If I turn the other cheek, do I become an enabler? If I give to the one who asks (and asks again), am I simply encouraging their undisciplined life? Jesus' answer seems to be, "Your business is to take care of your own soul rather than to run your neighbor's life. Do what is right with your resources, and leave it to your neighbor to handle his or hers."

Jesus insists on the law of love. That law is as indiscriminating as God's sunshine and rain, the world of nature that doesn't show preference for the nice people over the bad ones.

The Misuse of Religion

Although I hate to admit it, it's ironical that we can misuse religion as easily as we misuse food or drink or sex. Thus, Jesus dedicates a good piece of this sermon to our religious observances, such as prayer and fasting.

Our problem is our inclination to use valuable things to a cheap end: to pray and fast in order to win praise from those who observe us. If what we want is such attention, we'll get it, Jesus said, but we'll miss the divine favor. Our culture says, "If you've got it, flaunt it." Jesus said, "If you've got it, do your best to keep it a secret."

To help clarify his point, Jesus gave a pattern for prayer in what we call the Lord's Prayer or the "Our Father." It's quite simple and quite wonderful, so much so that we settle for quoting it rather than building on its pattern. Address God with reverence, pray for the Kingdom to come, ask for the needs of each day, ask for forgiveness even as you promise to forgive others, and pray for protection from "the evil one." Then, an addendum to the prayer

The Lord's Prayer

	Matthew 6:9-13	Luke 11:2-4
Address	Our Father who is in heaven	Father
First divine petition	Uphold the holiness of your name	Uphold the holiness of your name
Second divine petition	Bring in your kingdom	Bring in your kingdom
Third divine petition	So that your will is done on earth as it is in heaven	
First human petition	Give us the bread we need for today	Give us the bread we need for today
Second human petition	Forgive us for the ways we have wronged you, just as we forgive those who have wronged us	Forgive us our sins, for we also forgive everyone who has wronged us
Third human petition	Don't lead us into temptation, but resucue us from the evil one.	Don't lead us into temptation.

proper reminds us again to forgive others. Since this is the one element of the prayer that Jesus commented on, it must surely be uniquely important.

There are also our treasures! We work so hard for these benefits of earth, forgetting that they will inevitably pass away. We have this problem because our vision is poor, Jesus goes on to say. If our spiritual eyes were healthy, we would see the difference between the temporal and the eternal.

I see irony for the world in which I live when I read Jesus' words, "Therefore, don't worry and say, 'What are we going to eat?'" (6:31). Jesus' immediate audience was made up largely of people whose diets were exceedingly simple and often spare; obesity was not a prevailing problem. By comparison, observe how many of our contemporary social conversations discuss favorite restaurants or favorite foods or, on the other hand, diet programs.

Ultimately the issue is "God's kingdom and God's righteousness" (6:33). Why worry about tomorrow when tomorrow is such a temporary issue? If we seek God's kingdom and righteousness, all these matters that we worry about will be given to us in proper time. Then Jesus offers a bit of Jewish wisdom, delivered with humor: Why stop worrying about tomorrow? Because "each day has enough trouble of its own" (6:34).

We often think of this sermon as almost ethereal because of the high standards held out in the Beatitudes and in the appeal for sacrificing ourselves to others. At the same time, however, it is packed full of wonderfully down-to-earth insistence: "Don't judge, so that you won't be judged" (7:1). What good advice!

We generally read this verse with the thought of eventual divine judgment; that is, that God will judge us in the measure of our judgment of others. While this is true enough, the same principle is at work here on earth. People who judge others severely set themselves up for such judgment from others. However, although Jesus warned that this would be so, you may have observed that those who judge most freely are often startled when others judge them.

Jesus also makes clear that all of our human judgments are distorted by our human frailties. We see the faults of others through the obstructions in our own eyes, thus dissembling our perceptions. Jesus counsels us to take care of our own weaknesses, after which we'll be better able to be helpful to others—if we're asked!

At this point the sermon returns to the subject of prayer, particularly importunity in prayer. Here we get the theme in the language of Jesus: We should be ready to pray with the intensity and perseverance of asking, searching, and knocking. This intensity is not called for because God is reluctant. To the contrary, Jesus reminds us that God is more gracious toward our needs than even the most loving human parent.

However, an unspoken factor is at work: We must keep praying because there are obstacles to prayer. There are those things in our world, and often in our lives even as we pray, that prevent prayer from being answered or at the least that delay the answer. So we must continue to ask, to search, and to knock.

A Severe Word

The concluding paragraphs of this sermon have a severe quality. Jesus is often seen by our culture as so gentle and accepting as to be without standards. We get that picture because of his readiness to extend forgiveness and to offer a second chance. We see it particularly in the warmth of his welcome to sinners in his parables and in his readiness to associate with those elements of society that the professional religious of his day ostracized. However, Jesus was by no means indifferent to sin—the farthest thing from it—nor was he acquiescent in his expectations.

For example, listen to his warning against "false prophets": They dress like sheep, Jesus said, but "inside they're vicious wolves" (7:15). Beliefs have consequences, therefore one must examine fiercely the ideas that are offered in the religious and philosophical marketplace.

I think Jesus would have something to say about what is said to us in the commercial, political, and religious world today, a culture where sound bytes and bumper stickers are palmed off as thoughtful reasons. When our culture asks us to give our money, our time, our vote, or our dedication to that which appeals to our basest nature, we should know that however appealing the voices may be, they may be the voices of "vicious wolves," false prophets.

In Jesus' day, the false prophets worked on the street corner and, when possible, in the synagogue. Today they have easy access to our homes and automobiles and workplaces because we live in a multi-powered, almost inescapable communication system. Jesus warned specifically about those who dare to speak in his name. This is a hard saying. There are some, Jesus said, who on the day of judgment will seek to enter heaven, insisting that they have represented Jesus, even to the point of working miracles in his name. To these people Jesus will say, "I've never known you. Get away from me, you people who do wrong" (7:23).

I am not ready to attach this judgment to any persons or party. Jesus doesn't give us enough data to understand whom he might have in mind. I choose to accept his words as a kind of universal warning to all of us who claim to speak and work for the Kingdom, lay and clergy, realizing that we are susceptible to self-deception and can do presumably religious things with wrong motives.

At the least, this is Jesus' warning to all of us who follow him that we must live with such humility that we are always open to correction. There is no deception more dangerous than the self-deception that comes from religious motivation. This is why self-righteousness and evil words and deeds rear their heads in virtuous places.

Thus the Sermon on the Mount that began with the Beatitudes ("supreme blessedness") ends with an invitation couched in a warning. We can build our lives, Jesus said, in one of two ways: on sand (like a fool), so that when the storms come the house will be swept away; or on rock, so that however fierce the storm, the house will stand. Mind you, Jesus indicates that storms will come; life is like that. The issue is simply whether we are building in such a way that the storms hold no terror for us.

How do we do that? By hearing "these words of mine," Jesus said, "and [putting] them into practice" (7:24). That's practical religion, indeed, a body of faith that is secure from any storm that this life may bring.

Live the Story

The Sermon on the Mount is like a spiritual Mount Everest: Millions of us recognize its name, but few of us dare to approach its heights. Some of the loveliest declarations in this sermon are also the most challenging, in fact, the most frightening.

The sermon offers you an extraordinary way of life, one in which you're not afraid to be pure (some would call it naïve) in a world that constantly entices you to impurity. It offers a way of life whose quality is judged not simply by your outward conduct but more crucially by your thoughts within, which no one but God may ever know. Jesus introduces you to a life that finds blessing in the search for righteousness and, against all odds, in making peace.

This is a life in which you don't let slights or even intentional injuries upset you. It's a life not governed by the clothes you wear or the restaurants in which you eat. In the vernacular, "No sweat," or in biblical language, "Worry not; the pagans worry about these things." It's a call to the most serious religious living, yet one where you keep your piety a secret so people won't know how much you pray, how often you fast, or how much you give to your church and to the poor. At times it could be a lonely life because the gate is narrow and the road is difficult.

This way of life makes sense and offers deep happiness only if you can discern the kingdom of heaven as a present reality and draw strength and encouragement from it while trusting God for its ultimate fulfillment. If you can recognize the Kingdom around you, you are already blessed. If you cannot quite make it out, then offer the prayer of the man who told Jesus, "I have faith; help my lack of faith!" (Mark 9:24).

Consider your own spiritual Mount Everest. What would it take for you to go to a higher level? What will you do to increase your own faith in your daily living?

4.

Jesus Changes "Outsiders" Into "Insiders"

Matthew 8–12

Claim Your Story

C. S. Lewis, the renowned Christian apologist and author of the beloved *Chronicles of Narnia*, gave a speech some years ago at Kings College, University of London, entitled "The Inner Ring." Lewis spoke about the universal human longing to be a member of some inner circle or inner ring. Such exclusive circles can be found in all walks of life and work and leisure. Membership often carries tangible benefits, but the real attraction is "the delicious sense of secret intimacy."[1]

You know what he was talking about. Remember the reality of inner rings of childhood friendships with favored insiders and wounded outsiders? The division between those inside the ring and those longing to be inside the ring only grew more prominent as you moved through your teenage years.

As an adult, you've noticed that the appeal of being part of the inner circle reappears at the office or the factory or the club. Whatever your age and station, you undoubtedly remember those occasions when you enjoyed the wonderful feeling of being selected and included and those times when you felt the pain of being excluded.

The pattern of inner rings, with favored insiders and rejected outsiders, was a reality in Jesus' time, too. Those persons with power, wealth, good health, education, or social or religious prestige saw themselves and one another as members of the inner ring. Those persons who were powerless, poor, sick or crippled, uneducated, or socially or religiously unclean saw themselves and were seen by others as outsiders. Those outsiders surely ached to belong as most anyone would.

Jesus turned things upside down. His compassion and power touched the lives of people beyond the pale of privilege. In so doing, Jesus redefined what it means to be part of God's community then and now. Some people welcomed the new community; some were threatened by it, as is true today.

Where do you find yourself? Where do you want to belong?

Enter the Bible Story

I doubt that Jesus' original audience was ready for the transition from the Sermon on the Mount to life in the valley. They had just been marveling about the power of Jesus' words, how—unlike the usual Scripture expositors—he spoke with "authority." As they stepped from the classroom of the mountainside, they were approached by life in its worst guise, a leper. For persons so afflicted, leprosy was a kind of living death. At that time, lepers were compelled by law to live in isolation, even to the point of warning people when they were in shouting distance.

Jesus' Power Touches Outsiders

However, a particular leper let none of the usual restrictions get in his way. He was made bold by despair. He thrust the issue on Jesus: If you want to, he said, you could make me clean. That is, he was asking Jesus what God's will was for his life: to be a leper or to be made whole. Jesus took him at his dare. "I want to," he answered, "become clean."

Jesus completed the miracle in a rather routine way, instructing the cleansed leper to follow the law of his culture by reporting to the proper authorities; but the man was not to tell of the miracle that had happened. Why not? Apparently because Jesus was keeping a low profile. Even leprosy was part of the status quo. All kinds of regulations circumscribed it. If all the lepers were healed, the people of that culture wouldn't have known how to handle it.

Then there's one of the loveliest stories of Jesus' ministry. It involves a man with extraordinary faith. A military man, one who had reached the rank of centurion, appealed to Jesus to heal his seriously ill servant. However, on grounds of his unworthiness, he rejected Jesus' offer to come to his home. Besides, such a trip was unnecessary. The centurion understood the lines by which authority worked by observing how it was in the military. He reasoned that Jesus had such authority over all that was evil that he needed to do no more than to say the word and the servant would be well—and it was so.

Jesus said he hadn't seen this kind of faith in Israel among God's chosen people. He said that many would come from the non-Jewish world to eat at God's kingdom, while those in the usual religious community would be outside. We might rightly say that the centurion was in the faith line of the magi, Gentiles who had come early to recognize Jesus.

In any event, Jesus was making clear that God's kingdom was going to reach far beyond the usual ethnic boundaries. Most people in Jesus' day believed that their ethnic group was favored over others. They were uneasy if outsiders seemed to enjoy divine favor. They preferred a kingdom where God was prejudiced on their behalf.

Some boundaries are especially difficult to breach. It proved so when Jesus worked a miracle in the country of the Gadarenes, delivering two demon-possessed men who lived among the tombs, so violent that people couldn't travel the adjoining road. Jesus healed the men, sending the demons to a nearby herd of pigs that promptly rushed over the cliff and into the sea.

When the citizens of the country saw what had happened to their economy, they begged Jesus to leave their territory. The redemption of two human lives didn't seem so important to them as their local industry. I don't think this was the only time when people decided that pigs are more important than people. It's hard to bring in the kingdom of God when it affects someone's profit line, career, or political influence unfavorably.

It's unnerving to see how much trouble can develop when good is being done. We idealists often think that everyone will rejoice in human gain, but every gain comes at some price. So it is that when Jesus forgave a paralyzed man's sins before healing him, religious purists objected. They noted that no one but God could forgive sins, so Jesus was doing something only God can do. His act was therefore blasphemous, by their reasoning.

Across the Testaments

Matthew and the Hebrew Scriptures

Citation in Matthew	Old Testament Reference
Matthew 8:2-4 Jesus heals a leper.	Leviticus 14 Ritual of purification for lepers
Matthew 8:11-12 Jesus speaks of a coming banquet.	Isaiah 25:1-9 Vision of the banquet at the end of time
Matthew 8:17 Jesus' healing is as the work of the servant.	Isaiah 53:4 Work of the servant
Matthew 9:20-22 Jesus heals a woman's chronic bleeding.	Leviticus 15:25-30 Women with chronic bleeding are unclean.
Matthew 9:18-19, 23-25 Jesus restores a girl to life.	1 Kings 17:22; 2 Kings 4:32-35 Elijah restores the widow's son to life. Elisha restores a boy to life.
Matthew 11:4-6 Jesus responds to John's question.	Isaiah 26:19; 29:18-19; 35:5-6; 42:7; 61:1 Visions of God's liberating power
Matthew 11:10 John the Baptist as promised messenger	Malachi 3:1 The coming messenger
Matthew 12:1-8 Jesus interprets the sabbath.	Exodus 20:8-11; 1 Samuel 21:1-6 One of the Ten Commandments David eats the bread of Presence.
Matthew 12:18-21 Jesus fulfills the role of the servant.	Isaiah 42:1-4 A prophecy of the servant of God
Matthew 12:38-41 Jesus refers to the sign of Jonah.	Jonah 1-4 Jonah in the belly of a great fish
Matthew 12:42 Something greater than Solomon	1 Kings 10 Queen of Sheba visits King Solomon.

Jesus answered them with their own theology. They taught that such a person was ill because of his sins, so when Jesus healed the man after forgiving his sins, he was demonstrating that by their reasoning he had the power to forgive sins.

As Matthew 9 unfolds, we sense already that the actions and teachings of our Lord are leading to crucifixion. The miracle to which I've just referred, with its implications for the inferred claims of our Lord, arouses opposition. Then, as Jesus ate with Matthew the tax collector and his assortment of sinner friends, the Pharisees challenged Jesus' disciples: Why does your Master eat with such people? Lines were being drawn, and with every such delineation another step was made toward Calvary.

Meanwhile, however, Jesus continued to minister to people. A man asked Jesus to heal his daughter. While they were en route to the man's home, a woman with a longstanding illness reached out simply to touch Jesus' robe, confident that such a touch would bring healing, as indeed it did. However, there was another issue. Her kind of illness had issues of uncleanness by the Mosaic law, so it isn't surprising that she sought healing anonymously.

Jesus' healing was also a kind of parable-in-action, suggesting that even the poorest reaching out to God is honored, including even that which on the surface seems hardly more than superstition. God judges by the heart, not by detached logic.

Jesus healed blind men and a mute man. Pharisees explained the latter case as the ruler of demons casting out demons, a further sign of the growing animosity from religious leaders. However, Jesus was undeterred. He went through cities and villages, teaching in synagogues, "announcing the good news of the kingdom, and healing every disease and every sickness" (9:35), because of the compassion that compelled him. I suspect that the more persons Jesus healed, the more sick came flocking to him, so that he told his disciples to pray for the Lord of the harvest to send more recruits.

Jesus Sends Out the Disciples

It is instructive that the next recorded act is Jesus' empowering of his twelve disciples. At this point, Matthew lists their names, a few of which are memorable but the majority hardly known to us. Nonetheless, the

Master claimed them and gave them authority—the quality the crowds saw in Jesus. Jesus had authority, and he granted authority to those who worked with him. You and I should remember this, should know that when we seek to serve in Christ's name, we serve with his power.

The rest of Chapter 10 is a commissioning service, so to speak, for the Twelve. In some ways, the secrets of the authority we see in Jesus were demonstrated in such matters as the utter commitment to God and to the Kingdom. With it was indifference to rejection and persecution.

Jesus impressed upon the disciples that the time was short. In truth, it always is. The Kingdom is long in coming, but each hour is crucial to its purposes. For Jesus, the road was leading to Calvary and there was no time to waste. The Kingdom's base was in Judaism and its Scriptures, so Jesus instructed the disciples to go to Israel first. If a community rejected their teaching, they were to shake the dust from their feet and move on. Jesus warned his disciples that they would face persecution, like sheep among wolves. This Kingdom business has its price!

I see two issues here. One, don't waste time on lost causes when there are so many tasks still to be done. Second, don't live in the failures of the past. Shake such off as the dust that it is.

I suspect that most of us live in cultures with enough surface Christianity that we are generally comfortable rather than persecuted. Perhaps if we tried more often and more clearly to be more thoroughly Christian, the culture would be less friendly to us. In any event, Jesus said, be afraid not of those who can destroy the body but of that which can destroy the soul.

A Question From John the Baptist

Early in our study we met John the Baptist, the hardiest of souls and the prophet most indifferent to the opinions and judgments of others. He knew who he was; he was the one who was to prepare the way for the Christ. When Jesus appeared, John gladly stepped aside.

However, the scene changes as we enter Chapter 11. John was in prison for daring to preach clearly against the conduct of a king; and in the loneliness and peril of the prison, he sought reassurance. He sent a few of

The Twelve Disciples in Matthew, Mark, Luke, and Acts

Matthew 10	Mark 3	Luke 6	Acts 1
Simon, who is called Peter	Peter, a name [Jesus] gave Simon	Simon, whom he named Peter	Peter
Andrew his brother	James	his brother Andrew	John
James the son of Zebedee	John (with James, Zebedee's sons, whom he nicknamed Boanerges, which means "sons of Thunder")	James	James
John his brother	Andrew	John	Andrew
Philip	Philip	Philip	Philip
Bartholomew	Bartholomew	Bartholomew	Thomas
Thomas	Matthew	Matthew	Bartholomew
Matthew the tax collector	Thomas	Thomas	Matthew
James the son of Alphaeus	James, Alphaeus' son	James the son of Alphaeus	James, Alphaeus's son
Thaddaeus	Thaddaeus	Simon, who was called a zealot	Simon the zealot
Simon the Cananaean	Simon the Cananaean	Judas the son of James	Judas, James' son
Judas, who betrayed Jesus	Judas Iscariot, who betrayed Jesus	Judas Iscariot, who became a traitor	

his remaining disciples to Jesus with a question: "Are you the one who is to come, or should we look for another?" (11:3).

Had John lost faith? Perhaps, his faith was being sorely tried. Probably several elements were at work. Certainly John's pain and his sense of personal defeat had to weaken his vigorous spirit. Also, I wonder to what degree John misunderstood, or limited, what Jesus Christ was to be and to do.

Did John, like the first disciples, think Jesus was to set up a physical kingdom for Judaism? If so, it was a small vision but an understandable one. If this was John's expectation, he had to be disappointed in what was happening in Jesus' work because it was already clear that Jesus was not putting together a political structure. John's ministry, like that of so many of the Hebrew prophets, had challenged the political leadership; however, Jesus seemed indifferent to that issue. He challenged the religious leaders but did so almost incidentally when those leaders criticized the work Jesus was doing.

Jesus' answer pointed John to the work Jesus was doing: healing the blind, the crippled, the lepers, and the deaf, and raising the dead. "The poor have good news proclaimed to them" (11:5). John had to have known all of this and quite possibly these were the very matters that left him bewildered. These works would make Jesus known for miracles and for compassion; but they wouldn't build a kingdom, not even in Israel. It is as if Jesus were saying, "Regardless of what you were expecting, *this* is who I am."

No doubt we twenty-first-century followers of Jesus and many potential followers have the same problem John had. We want Jesus to fit our expectations. We have ideas about what he should be politically, economically, and religiously. We can easily ask with John if he's the one. Well, as the guide in the Paris art gallery said to the woman who didn't like a masterpiece, "Madam, you don't judge this picture; the picture judges you." Our assignment is to measure up to Jesus, not to bring Jesus down to our wishes and expectations.

After John's disciples had left, Jesus made a grand declaration about the incomparable stature of John the Baptist and declared that he was the Elijah for their day. He condemned the fickle crowds for their readiness to discredit John and himself. Cities such as Bethsaida and Capernaum had seen many miracles from Jesus' ministry and had remained unchanged.

In truth, miracles rarely change minds for long. We make our soul-decisions on less glamorous but more sustained points, namely, on truth. Jesus credits us with being rational creatures and therefore with the ability to choose between truth and falsehood. He knows we have a readiness to give ourselves to the best.

Strange to say, however, our rationality is at its best when it maintains a quality of simplicity. Jesus thanked his Father that the wonders of the Kingdom are hidden from "the wise and intelligent" while God has shown them "to babies" (11:25). With that, Jesus extended again his offer to those "who are struggling hard and carrying heavy loads" (11:28). He had come to offer a better way for those who were willing to receive it.

Hostility to Jesus

Unfortunately, as Chapter 12 demonstrates, some preferred a heavy load, a load of their own making. The issue was with God's gift of the sabbath and how rightly to observe it. In this instance, the issue began with Jesus' disciples. As they walked through the wheat fields on a sabbath, they picked heads of grain and ate them. The Pharisees, who saw themselves as the sabbath police, immediately brought the matter to Jesus' attention. Jesus replied by pointing to places in the Hebrew Scriptures that justified the conduct of his disciples. Then, as if to give an object lesson, he proceeded to offend his critics even more by healing a man with a withered hand (12:9-14).

It was a showdown kind of case. Matthew writes, "Wanting to bring charges against Jesus, they asked, 'Does the Law allow a person to heal on the Sabbath?'" (12:10). Jesus answered with a question: If your animal falls into a pit on the sabbath, you'll bring it out, won't you? "So the Law allows a person to do what is good on the Sabbath" (12:12), and then Jesus healed the man. Neither the miracle nor Jesus' logic moved the Pharisees; they "went out and met in order to find a way to destroy Jesus" (12:14). If this was God's kingdom, they did not recognize it or wanted nothing of it.

The tension grew and spread. When Jesus healed a demon-possessed man who was also blind, the Pharisees credited the miracle to demonic power. Jesus, in turn, noted that no sin is as serious as "insulting the Holy Spirit" (12:31-32). We will be held in judgment for our words (12:36-37).

About the Scripture

The Pharisees and Scribes

The Pharisees constituted one of the most important Jewish groups during New Testament times. The Gospel portrayal of them is largely negative, presenting them most of the time as hypocrites and opponents of Jesus. Biblical scholars remind us that all four of the Gospels were written some decades after the time of Jesus (though certainly drawing on early tradition). Because of that fact, scholars caution today's readers that we cannot always be sure how much the Gospels reflect a conflict between Jesus and the Pharisees of his time and how much the Gospels reflect a conflict between the early church and the Pharisees of that time.

The name *pharisees* can mean "the separated ones," those who sought holiness by adherence to the Law and by avoiding those things regarded as unclean. The Pharisees were the spiritual descendants of the Hasidim, the Jewish group. They were zealous for the Law, and they emerged at the time of the Maccabean Revolt (166–159 B.C.), when the high priests were seen as too accommodating to the intrusion of Hellenistic ways into Judaism.

Central to the teaching of the Pharisees was the belief in the two-fold Law: the written and the oral Torah. Sometimes viewed as legalistic, it might be fairer to say that the Pharisees had a zeal for legal debate and the continuing relevance of the Law in changing situations. Like Jesus, and unlike the priestly Sadducees, the Pharisees believed in life after death and the resurrection of the body. Generally speaking, they were highly respected leaders in Jerusalem and other communities.

While some scribes copied biblical texts, scribes also functioned as lawyers, clerks, and legal council for various clients, including the Sanhedrin and some Pharisees. The authority of the scribes was delegated or derivative. That is, they interpreted existing law; they did not create it. When Jesus is distinguished from the scribes as one who had authority (Matthew 7:29), the implication is that he as the Messiah had royal authority to make law.

When the legal experts and Pharisees asked Jesus for a sign (a peculiar request, in light of the miracles he had been performing in their presence and that they had so often rejected), Jesus replied that the only sign they would receive would be the sign of Jonah. For those who listened perceptively, Jesus' answer was a reference to his coming death and resurrection.

Somewhere in the midst of these sharp exchanges, Jesus was told that his mother and brothers were waiting to speak with him. However, Jesus "stretched out his hand toward his disciples and said, 'Look, here are my mother and my brothers. Whoever does the will of my Father who is in heaven is my brother, sister, and mother'" (12:49-50).

Jesus was defining the nature of the Kingdom community, a definition that at the same moment became more inclusive and more exclusive. More inclusive in that anyone who desires can enter; but more exclusive in that it shuts out even those closest to us if they refuse the Kingdom's demands.

Live the Story

The invitation Jesus issued is in sharp contrast to the siren songs of many "inner rings." Do you want to belong to the community Jesus brought into being? Are you willing to live counter-culturally so that you can be part of that community? What would you need to change in your life?

Some of us are privileged socially or economically, but we are not the only ones Christ welcomes. The Kingdom embraces the poor, the needy, the outcast—outsiders of every sort and stripe. Who is it that you need to welcome into the Kingdom? Who are the ones your congregation needs to welcome? Who are the ones you need to stop ignoring?

Jesus invites you to belong to a marvelous community. Membership has its benefits, but membership in the fellowship of Jesus also has its costs. For Jesus the price of the Kingdom was the cross. If you take Jesus seriously, that may cause misunderstanding. Some good and well-meaning people may think you're going too far. Faithful discipleship may sometimes mean that you have to move outside your comfort zone and, in the process, ruffle some feathers.

Can you imagine what risks you might face if you took Jesus with utmost seriousness? Are you willing to be upsetting to someone else for the sake of God's inclusive community?

Take a few minutes to make a list of the groups that you have been part of. Then make a list of the groups you wanted to be part of but from which you were excluded. Ask yourself: What was it that made belonging to those groups attractive? Was the reality of membership satisfying? What was missing? What does Jesus offer that you need or want? Who else might you invite to be part of the Kingdom inaugurated by Jesus?

Offer a short prayer, giving thanks to God for welcoming you with open arms.

[1]From *The Weight of Glory and Other Addresses*, Walter Hooper, editor (MacMillan Publishing Company, Inc., 1975); page 100.

5.

Jesus Proclaims the Kingdom of Heaven

Matthew 13–22

Claim Your Story

I'll bet you've seen one of those line drawings, perhaps in a psychology textbook, that contain two images, for example, the figure of a lovely young woman and the wrinkled face of an aged woman. If someone told you that you were looking at a drawing of a young woman, that's probably what you saw. If, instead, someone told you that you were looking at a drawing of an aged woman, then that's probably what you saw.

Remember how difficult it was to switch from one perception to the other and how it was virtually impossible to see both images simultaneously? All of us sometimes operate on the basis of preconceived notions, seeing only what we expect to see or seeing only what we want to see.

When have you looked forward to something—a gift, a relationship, a promotion, a vacation, or a special event—so much that you thought about it every waking hour? Did it turn out to be what you wanted, or were you surprised by something different than what you expected? How did that feel?

The people in Jesus' day who were potentially the best scholars, the scribes and Pharisees, found it most difficult to grasp his message. The reason is probably simple: Jesus wasn't what they were looking for, so they missed him.

Do you have such preconceived notions about Jesus that you find it difficult to hear what he is saying? When you hear mention of the kingdom of heaven, what comes to mind? A place? a concept? a vision of the future? a way of living? When Jesus speaks of the kingdom of heaven, do your presuppositions prevent you from hearing what he is saying?

Enter the Bible Story

The Gospel of Matthew emphasizes Jesus' role as a teacher. Look at the teaching itself. We note often that Jesus taught through parables; but the parables confused many, including the disciples. "Why do you use parables when you speak to the crowds?" they asked. Jesus answered, "This is why I speak to the crowds in parables: although they see, they don't see; and although they hear, they don't really hear or understand" (13:10, 13).

Rather than being troubled that many weren't getting his message, Jesus seemed to take it for granted. Jesus said that his work was like that of a farmer spreading seed. Most of it proves unproductive, but that which finds good soil brings forth abundantly. Apparently he was satisfied with this inefficient system of "farming."

Jesus explained in another parable that after good seed has been planted in the world's field, "an enemy" comes and plants weeds among the wheat, thus endangering the entire crop. What were his followers to do about this danger? Nothing, Jesus said; wait until "the harvest," when God will separate the weeds from the grain (13:24-30). This kind of teaching doesn't seem threatening; indeed, it suggests that there's no hurry. Things will work out in time. It may leave us wondering exactly how we're to help bring Jesus' kingdom to pass in our day and time.

The Kingdom of Heaven Is Full of Surprises

The Kingdom, Jesus said, is like a mustard seed, so small yet eventually a bush as large as a small tree, where birds can nest in its branches. The Kingdom is also like yeast: Hide a little in a bushel of wheat flour, and it will eventually work its way through the whole large unit. The Kingdom is like a net that gathers all kinds of fish. Throw away the bad fish, and keep the good. So it will be, Jesus said, "at the end of the present age" (13:47-50).

It seems, then, that the kingdom of heaven is not a massive, overwhelming enterprise but one influential beyond its size. Yet this Kingdom is so much to be desired that it's like a treasure found in a field; the person discovering it sells everything to buy the field. It's like a merchant who has wanted for years to find a choice pearl. When he finds it, he sells everything he owns in order to get that pearl (13:44-46).

These parables of the Kingdom make one question the way we've gone about doing church. Jesus seems to say that the measure is not in the number of fish in the net but those in the number that are good. It isn't our size (as in yeast or in mustard seed) but in the purity and influence of our witness.

So why would any of these parables be reason to see Jesus as a dangerous teacher? Leaders of the Jewish religious establishment might have decided that whatever Jesus had in mind, they were the bad guys in his parables and sometimes in his direct statements, which of course they didn't like. As for the disciples, and all of Jesus' followers since, the point seems to be "You've taken on a huge assignment. It's not for the faint of heart."

No wonder, then, that when Jesus returned to his hometown, his old associates remembered that they knew his whole family and they weren't impressed. Thus Jesus "was unable to do many miracles there because of their disbelief" (13:53-58).

Elsewhere, however, miracles seemed to come easily. So Jesus fed five thousand with five loaves of bread and two fish. After the crowds had gone and Jesus had spent time alone in a mountain praying, he rejoined his disciples by walking on the water, a matter that, not surprisingly, caused those on the boat to say, "You must be God's Son" (14:33). When they came to Gennesaret on the other side of the lake, the ill asked if they could simply "touch the edge of his clothes. Everyone who touched him was cured" (14:34-36). The miracles that were almost non-existent in Nazareth were commonplace in Gennesaret.

This contrast between doubters and believers continues. When the "Pharisees and legal experts" went to Jesus, it was only to find fault—and they found it (15:1-9). However, when a Canaanite woman appealed for healing for her severely afflicted daughter, she received it, even against the odds (15:21-28).

Large crowds with every kind of illness followed Jesus, and Jesus healed them all (15:29-31). Later, he fed another massive crowd, this time four thousand (15:32-39). However, the cynical leaders of the Pharisees and Sadducees asked for a sign from heaven, a request that Jesus scorned (16:1-4).

People get what they're seeking. Those who came to Jesus seeking healing went away whole, and those who were looking for ways to destroy Jesus steadily built their case for judgment and death.

In some ways, Jesus' disciples did little better than the transient crowds in understanding his message. Like most of us, they heard what they wanted or expected to hear. When Jesus asked his disciples who they perceived him to be, Peter replied with the grand confession upon which the church still stands: "You are the Christ, the Son of the living God" (16:13-16).

However, when Jesus told his disciples that he had to go to Jerusalem to suffer many things and be "killed and raised on the third day," Peter, who moments before served as the grand spokesman of the Kingdom, couldn't accept what Jesus said. The idea that Jesus would be killed drowned out the promise that he would be raised on the third day.

At that point, Jesus challenged his disciples: "All who want to come after me should say no to themselves, take up their cross, and follow me" (16:24). A kingdom is coming, but it is for cross-bearers. Even Jesus' best disciples, then and now, find it hard to understand the cross. We like the end product, the mass of wheat that becomes bread and the mustard seed that becomes a flourishing plant; but we don't like the fact that the yeast is lost in the process of the bread or that the mustard seed must die in order for the plant to grow.

For the disciples, every day with Jesus was another day of learning. It wasn't simply the established hours of teaching. The very idea of being a disciple was that one was with the teacher at all times so that any moment, any event, any apparently idle conversation might become a teaching moment.

An Illuminating Experience

Peter, James, and John experienced a unique seminar. Jesus took them to a mountain where he was "transformed in front of them," radiant as the sun (17:2). Moses and Elijah (symbolizing the Law and the Prophets, the basic body of the Hebrew Scriptures) appeared, talking with Jesus. Then, just as suddenly, the disciples were again alone with Jesus, hearing a voice from the cloud, "This is my Son whom I dearly love. I am very pleased with him. Listen to him!" (17:5). The disciples, understandably,

Matthew and the Hebrew Scriptures

Citation in Matthew	Old Testament Reference
Matthew 15:30-31 Jesus heals the mute, the maimed, the lame, and the blind.	*Isaiah 35:5-6* In the promised new age, God will heal the blind, the deaf, the lame, and the mute.
Matthew 17:3 Moses and Elijah (Law-giver and prophet) appear beside Jesus at his Transfiguration.	*Exodus 24:12—34:35* Moses encounters God on Mount Sinai. God speaks out of a cloud. Moses' face becomes luminous.
Matthew 20:22-23 The cup that Jesus will drink	*Isaiah 51:17; Jeremiah 25:15;* *Lamentations 4:21* The bitter wine of suffering
Matthew 21:12-13 Jesus cleanses the Temple.	*Isaiah 56:7* "My house shall be called a house of prayer." *Jeremiah 7:11* The Temple has become "a den of robbers."

were terrified. They had been admitted to a moment of eternal glory, the kind of scene that would later be amplified in the Book of Revelation.

Their experience was a moment of unforgettable instruction, but it was followed by another teaching moment that was valuable but also painful. A father whose son was tragically afflicted had sought help from the disciples who were left behind when Jesus, Peter, James, and John went to the mountain; but they were helpless. Jesus, the teacher, became Jesus the frustrated teacher. "How long will I put up with you?" he chided the disciples before healing the boy. The disciples asked Jesus his secret, and he answered, "Faith."

Jesus turned again to his metaphor of the mustard seed. The mustard seed is small, but it has power hidden inside waiting to express itself. We're still dull to the potential in God's gift of faith.

Who Is the Greatest?

Sometimes Jesus' teaching came by way of questions from the disciples. This time they asked, "Who is the greatest in the kingdom of heaven?" (18:1). I don't believe I'm being unfair to the disciples when I suggest that they were anticipating that perhaps Jesus would say, "You are the greatest, you who have followed me as my closest disciples." I say this on the basis of the several instances where the disciples showed themselves to be ambitious men, expecting honor and promotion. I'm sure Jesus shocked them by his answer.

Jesus "called a little child over to sit among the disciples, and said, 'I assure you that if you don't turn your lives around and become like this little child, you will definitely not enter the kingdom of heaven'" (18:2-3). It was a hard saying, a rejection of their ambition and a counter-intuitive way to build a kingdom. Jesus wasn't looking for go-getters who would scramble for top positions but for disciples who were willing to become like children—scuffed-knee, smudged-face, unpretentious children.

Jesus proceeded to emphasize the importance of the individual soul. If we cause "these little ones who believe in me to trip and fall into sin," it would be better to have a huge stone tied to us and be drowned (18:6-9). Jesus wants us to pay attention to the least and the lost. If just one sheep is lost, the shepherd will search till he finds it. God is the same way with us (18:10-14). We can treat one another in the same way, too. If someone sins against you, go to that person, seeking to win them back (18:15-20).

Peter, always raising the kinds of questions you and I would have raised if we had been there, then asked how many times we should forgive. Should we do so, perhaps, "as many as seven times?" Jesus told one of his parables where the arithmetic was so ridiculous that Peter must have wondered why he asked (me, too). We have been forgiven, Jesus said, in such extravagant measure that there could be no hope of our ever repaying, so how dare we hesitate to forgive others their comparatively minor debts to us?

Topsy-turvy Teachings

In the teachings that follow, and in incidents that become teachings, Jesus continues to upset our usual ways of thinking. In the first-century world, divorce for men was almost as simple as declaring they desired it. However, Jesus raised a whole new standard (19:1-12). In that world, children were most surely to be seen and not heard, but Jesus gave them precedence and made them examples of the Kingdom life (19:13-15).

A man of obvious wealth asked how he could have eternal life. Jesus pointed the man to what he already knew and was pretty much doing—the commandments. When the man pressed further, Jesus invited him to give his wealth to the poor and to follow him. At that point, the man realized that he wasn't that interested in eternal life, not when it cost so much in this transient life! (19:16-22).

Jesus' disciples seemed almost as troubled by Jesus' answer as was the rich man. When Jesus said that it will be hard for a rich person to enter the kingdom of heaven, the disciples "were stunned. 'Then who can be saved?' they asked" (19:25). They equated economic success with spiritual favor.

Jesus then unnerved them still further with a parable about a landowner who began hiring day laborers early in the morning, promising them the conventional day's wages. Throughout the day, the landowner continued hiring until an hour before day's end. At checkout time, he gave all the workers the same amount, which was pay for a full day's work no matter how long they had worked. Jesus was teaching grace, not economics; but the disciples (again, like us) found it easier to understand a God of *quid pro quo* than a God of great and generous heart (20:1-16).

Once again, Jesus told the disciples that he would be arrested, crucified, and raised on the third day; but they didn't understand. The mother of James and John appealed that her sons be key leaders in Jesus' kingdom, at his right hand and left. When the other ten heard of the request, they were predictably offended. Jesus explained that his Kingdom would be different. Those who desired to be great should plan on being servants (20:20-28). The disciples still didn't get it. In case you haven't noticed, most of us today are still finding it hard to get.

The eternal drama was now moving rapidly to its climax. Jesus arranged to enter Jerusalem, not simply as a walking teacher, but riding on a donkey's colt instead of a beast of privilege. It was a procession that could have seemed humorous, a burlesque of a ruler's entrance, perhaps, as if Jesus were deliberately mocking the customary displays of power. Nevertheless, the common people were in awe. In their love for Jesus, they spread their clothes and palm branches on the road before him (21:1-11).

At this point, Jesus did an impolitic thing. He condemned the commercialism of religion and the exploitation of the Temple for private gain, driving out the merchants and moneychangers (21:12-17). Not surprisingly, the chief priests and elders challenged Jesus, asking on what authority was he doing these things.

Jesus deflected their question with a counter question and then told a parable about two sons. This time he also interpreted the parable as well because it was aimed precisely at the religious leaders, and Jesus made sure they got the point (21:28-32). Jesus then told another parable, aimed again at the professional religious leaders (21:33-46). This one was quite horrifying in its directness and its conclusion. When the chief priests and Pharisees heard it, "they knew Jesus was talking about them. They were trying to arrest him, but they feared the crowds, who thought he was a prophet" (21:45).

However, Jesus wasn't finished. As the wrath of his opponents mounted, he told still another story aimed again at the religious leaders (22:1-14). Jesus said that a king prepared a wedding party for his son. However, the guests refused to come—an unbelievable response to make to a king. The king, with extraordinary graciousness for a monarch, sent other servants to press the invitation; but the invited guests "paid no attention." The king then sent his soldiers to punish the ingrates and sent his servants to bring in everyone they could find. However, even such a broad invitation did not excuse a person who came without wedding clothes (22:11). Gracious as is God's gift, one still must accept the standards of entrance.

So the "Pharisees met together to find a way to trap Jesus in his words" (22:15). One almost pities these leaders who were so dull that they continued to pursue their inane course. Jesus fielded one question after another, each one frustrating his enemies still further. The climax about which Jesus had warned his disciples had come near.

Live the Story

How does all of this apply to you? What are you thinking about the kingdom of heaven now? Have your previous ideas been modified or confirmed? What do you find appealing about the Kingdom? What makes you uncomfortable? What gets in the way of you adopting a Kingdom way of life?

What does the Kingdom Jesus proclaimed require of you? What are you doing to participate in building God's Kingdom? What changes will that entail? How do you live out the gospel in a culture that glories in the material and sees the spiritual only as a means to an end? Is there any hope in a grain of mustard seed or a bit of yeast? Are you ready, like the merchant in Jesus' parable, to sell everything to get this gem of life?

Take a few moments to talk these matters over with God, sharing your concerns, confusions, doubts, and hopes.

6.

How Do We Live
for the Future Now?

Matthew 23–25

Claim Your Story

What can you tell me about tomorrow? Our desire to get advance information about the future is almost insatiable; and it touches every area of life, from who will play in the Super Bowl to the prospects of political parties in the next election.

Especially, we speculate on the big questions, those having to do with the welfare of our souls and of our universe. Will the world someday come to an end? If so, when? Will there be advance warning? Is our planet in danger of greater physical disasters than it has ever yet known? If so, when will that be? Is there anything specific you should do to prepare for such a happening?

I expect that human beings have been asking questions like these for as long as we have existed; they seem built into our DNA. We shouldn't be surprised, therefore, that the disciples brought such questions to Jesus.

Enter the Bible Story

In our last study, the Pharisees were questioning Jesus in every way possible in the hope of finding a way to discredit him and to diminish his popularity with the common people. However, Jesus met each twist of logic or clever argument with such ease that his opponents found themselves losing ground in every encounter. At last it came to a place where "nobody dared to ask him anything" (22:46).

As Jesus' opponents quietly moved away to plan their next maneuver, Jesus directed his attention "to the crowds and his disciples" (23:1). He talked to them about the people who had been trying to destroy him, reminding the crowds that the Pharisees had a position of honor and authority. They occupied "Moses' seat," that is, they were the premier interpreters of the Hebrew law. Unfortunately, their conduct wasn't as good as their teaching. Pay attention to what they teach, Jesus said, but "don't do what they do" (23:3).

The Pharisees From Generation to Generation

There's a little of the Pharisee in all of us, and a lot of the Pharisee in most of us. It is much easier to describe how others should live than to live with such wisdom and integrity ourselves. Of course it's not entirely to our discredit or to that of the Pharisees that we don't always live up to our professions and expectations. Theories are hard to put into practice. Worse yet, sometimes our theories make us blind to our own practices.

So it was that the Pharisees became indifferent to the needs of others and quite absorbed in the honors being paid to them. As is the nature of experts, the Pharisees became fascinated with philosophical hair-splitting while they lost sight of the very principles that undergirded all their theories. Thus they would pay a tithe on the few cups of spices they raised in their backyard, while they forgot "the more important matters of the Law: justice, peace, and faith" (23:23).

I feel sad each time I read about the Pharisees. They meant well. They were utterly sincere. They worked overtime at their faith, but they missed Jesus when he came. They should have been the first to recognize and endorse him. Instead, they became his most intense enemies.

What saddens me still more is that over the centuries we followers of Jesus have so often acted like Pharisees. Protestant or Catholic, liberal or conservative, first-century or twenty-first, we continue to major in minors. We lose Christ in some ecclesiastical bypath just as the Pharisees lost the sabbath in how many steps they could walk on that holy day.

No wonder, then, that Jesus finished his passionate declaration about the Pharisees by weeping over Jerusalem (23:37-39). Jerusalem was not only the City of David, the symbol of their government in the days when they were a free people, it was also the setting for their Temple and the place to which the people came at the high holy seasons.

Jerusalem symbolized Israel's national calling, their reason for existence, their moral authority, and their place among the nations. However, it was also the city that killed "the prophets and [stone] those who were sent" to them (23:37). Now Jerusalem was only days away from crucifying their Messiah.

What Does the Future Hold?

As Jesus and the disciples were leaving the Temple, the disciples drew Jesus' attention to the wonders of the complex. They were right in being impressed. The Temple had been in the process of being built for over a generation and was probably not yet complete at the time Jesus and his disciples visited there.

Some of the stones were almost forty feet long, and their green-white color made them shimmer in the sunlight to a point of blinding. The Temple itself was built on a man-made plateau 1,000 feet square. The area surrounding it held great porches, each marked by grand pillars so that the approaches to the complex were worthy of what was to follow.

It was breathtaking, no doubt about it; but Jesus answered, "Do you see all these things? I assure that no stone will be left on another. Everything will be demolished" (24:2). This got the disciples' attention. As they looked at the huge stones and the sheer grandeur of the structure, they had to wonder at Jesus' brusque dismissal. However, like all human creatures they wanted to know when such things would happen. So taking Jesus aside (probably reasoning that this was information only for select hearers like themselves), they asked him a handful of questions: "Tell us, when will these things happen. What will be the sign of your coming and the end of the age?" (24:3).

Readers of the Gospel of Matthew have been trying ever since to determine which of the questions Jesus was answering at which point in the verses that follow. Without a doubt, some of what Jesus said was fulfilled in 70 A.D. when the Roman armies devastated Jerusalem. At that time, the invaders made at least a good start on the prediction that "no stone will be left on another"; and what little they left unfinished was finished in succeeding centuries of invasions.

Matthew and the Hebrew Scriptures

Citation in Matthew	Old Testament Reference
Matthew 23:5 "They make extra-wide prayer bands for their arms and long tassels for their clothes."	*Exodus 13:9; Deuteronomy 6:8; 11:18* Phylacteries are small boxes containing Scripture quotations tied to the forehead and arms.
	Numbers 15:38-41; Deuteronomy 22:12 The wearing of tassels
Matthew 23:23-34 Jesus condemns the Pharisees for tithing on household spices but neglecting larger issues of justice.	*Deuteronomy 14:22* A tithe of the annual seed
Matthew 23:24 Jesus satirizes the Pharisees who "filter out an ant but swallow a camel."	*Leviticus 11:14; 41-43; Deuteronomy 14:7* Large and small animals deemed unclean
Matthew 24:25 Jesus borrows language from the Book of Daniel	*Daniel 9:27; 11:31; 12:11* Alludes to the persecutions of Antiochus IV
Matthew 24:30 The Son of Man	*Daniel 7:13-14* A vision of the Son of Man coming on clouds
Matthew 24:37-38 Behavior before the Flood	*Genesis 6–7* Noah and the Flood

What of the questions concerning the time of Jesus' return and the end of the age? These are the questions that fascinate us, as in fact they have fascinated every generation. When Paul was writing to the new believers at Thessalonica barely a generation after the Crucifixion and the Resurrection (and before the destruction of Jerusalem), they were wondering if theirs was the time of the end.

People thought that surely the time had come in the year 1000; the figure itself seemed ominous. Thousands of Americans thought the time had come in 1843 through the preaching of William Miller, and most of us remember the increased speculation that came when our calendar approached the new millennium and the year 2000. I have heard cases made on a vast variety of political, international, and cultural conditions, as well as phenomena of nature, to prove that the end times had come.

What Do We Know About the Return of Christ?

So what conclusions can we draw from what Jesus said? Let me declare that I believe that our Lord Christ will return some day. There is a place in our celebration of Holy Communion where we declare, "Christ has died; Christ is risen; Christ will come again." Each time I speak those words, I do so with glad vigor and with deep conviction. I believe Christ will come again.

"But when?" someone asks. I answer, "I don't know, and I don't think I really care to know. It's none of my business and none of yours, either." If there is anything that Jesus made utterly clear about his return it is that "nobody knows when that day or hour will come, not the heavenly angels and not the Son. Only the Father knows" (24:36). Those are the words of Jesus as recorded in the Gospel of Matthew. I think it is presumptuous, perhaps even heretical, for us to intrude on divine knowledge by estimating dates that we've been told are not our privilege.

Jesus then made his point still clearer by drawing an analogy from the time of Noah. In the days before the Flood, people were "eating and drinking, marrying and giving in marriage, until the day Noah entered the ark. They didn't know what was happening until the flood came" (24:38-39). Why was it that the people of Noah's time didn't know a flood was coming? Because life was proceeding in such normal fashion, they were "eating and drinking" (normal, proper conduct) and "marrying and giving in marriage" (doing just what humans are supposed to do, legitimately looking toward the future).

The people didn't know the Flood was coming because everything was as it had always been. If anything political, cultural, or spiritual was different, it was only a matter of degree; and degrees of difference are almost impossible to measure, since we humans are inclined to think of our own times as unique in their goodness or their badness.

Jesus didn't leave his followers without counsel, however. First, he compared us with servants who have been left in charge of the master's house during his absence. Under such circumstances some servants will take advantage of their master's absence, abusing the master's trust. Under such circumstances, Jesus said, the master "will come on a day when they're not expecting him, at a time they couldn't predict" (24:50).

Second, then he told a parable about a wedding feast, a scene common to his first-century hearers. A wedding was an event important to the entire village, but it wasn't announced for a certain hour or a certain date. The arrival of the bridegroom was possible over an extended period, which was part of the excitement and frivolity of the occasion.

In Jesus' parable, ten bridesmaids were planning to be part of the grand event. All of them were qualified and invited, and all of them were at least somewhat prepared because they had brought their lamps in case the bridegroom came at night.

Five of them, however, had brought an extra supply of oil. For this foresight, Jesus called them wise. They had kept alert because they realized that they didn't "know the day or the hour" (25:13). They were not wise because by some remarkable scholarship they had discovered the time of the bridegroom's coming. They were wise because by simple love and commitment they had made sure they would be there whenever the bridegroom's coming might be.

Then Jesus underlined the point with still another story. A man of considerable resources was leaving on a trip. He entrusted his investments to his servants, giving five talents to one, two to another, and one to a third, according to each servant's ability. (A talent was a monetary unit worth more than fifteen years' wages for a laborer).

When the man returned, the servant with five talents had gotten five more. The one with two talents had gotten two more. These two men demonstrated that they had used their time and ability in a way and a degree that pleased the master. However, the third servant hid his talent and returned it to his master with no gain. The servant defended himself by saying that he knew his master was a demanding sort. His master dismissed him without mercy because he hadn't used the opportunity that had been entrusted to him.

To let an opportunity go unused is to misuse it. We don't know how long the master will be gone; but when he returns, he expects us to show that we have used the time profitably.

The time of the Master's return is none of our business. Our business is to take care of the Master's business until he returns. It's quite simple. That's why we have such a hard time with it.

How to Live for the Future

Matthew concludes his report of this special section of Jesus' teaching with a story that is straightforward and easy to understand but also encouraging and frightening. We're told from the outset that we are getting a preview of the judgment of the nations (25:32). Most of the time we seem to apply this story to our individual conduct—and rightly so. However, we need also to pause and consider what Jesus is saying specifically: that the nations of this earth will be judged for their policies.

At the judgment, Christ will separate them as sheep and goats, with the sheep to his right and the goats to his left. He will then say to those on his right, "Come, you who will receive good things from my Father. Inherit the kingdom that was prepared for you before the world began" (25:34).

Let me make two observations before proceeding further. Notice that we are back to the same language and the same figure of speech with which Matthew began: the figure of the Kingdom. John the Baptist prepared his audience for the coming of Jesus with the announcement that the kingdom of heaven was at hand, and Jesus preached from the beginning details of Kingdom life. As Jesus' trial and crucifixion drew near, he gave a Kingdom parable.

Further, note that this story involves God's eternal plan. God has had this end in mind since before the world began. That is, God's plan for our earth has always been a moral one. God's plan is structured in gracious justice, with concern for the weak and with expectation of responsibility from those who are strong.

So hear the details. The Kingdom is given to those who have fed Jesus when he was hungry, clothed him when he was naked, welcomed him as a stranger, visited him in prison, and took care of him in his need. The ones who are praised are astonished because they don't remember ever having extended such goodness to their Lord. He remembers the occasions, however: "I assure you that when you have done it for one of the least of these brothers and sisters of mine, you have done it for me" (25:40).

Then the king spoke to those on his left. The story is a mirror opposite. He ordered, "Get away from me." Why? Because when he was hungry, they gave him no food. When he was thirsty, they offered him no drink. When he was a stranger, they offered him no hospitality. When he was naked, they gave him no clothing. When he was sick and in prison, they did nothing for him.

Like the people on the right who had no memory of the listed kindnesses, these nations couldn't recall ever treating the king this way. After all, who would deny hospitality to a king? The king's answer was the same as before, with reverse data and results: "I assure you that when you haven't done it for one of the least of these, you haven't done it for me" (25:45).

Both of these dialogues are given in painstaking detail, like a children's story where the listeners can anticipate the lines before they're spoken. We will be judged not by our pious protestations or our stated religious observances. We will be judged by our care for those in need because those in need are our Lord's "brothers and sisters."

This parable in two acts challenges our thinking because it portrays a judgment of nations rather than of individuals. Most of us have been raised in an individualistic society, so we don't have the sense of the voluntary or compelled community that was characteristic of the first-century world.

Is the parable urging us to be a positive influence within our nations? This seems a stretch, since the first-century world was one in which people had essentially no influence on their governments. Are we to be a constant leaven-in-the-lump influence so that our individual conduct eventually becomes a national character? Whatever, of this much I am certain: My responsibility and yours is to extend to every individual the kind of love and concern we would extend if we knew that person was our Lord Christ because our Lord Christ thinks of each individual that way.

Live the Story

So what do you know about the future? Well, to begin with, you know that there is going to be a future. This is reassuring! Furthermore, let me tell you that God is concerned about the future and that God wants you to be concerned.

I believe, further, that you have a part in the shaping of the future. This is quite clear in the parable of the landowner who gave each of his workers resources to use in his absence. You are not simply an inhabitant of this planet, you are one of its shapers and makers; and God will judge you accordingly.

It is clear that God expects you to influence the future by your care of those who have less than you do, those who are disadvantaged by sickness or poverty or perhaps even by their sins and crimes that have brought them to prison. However, God doesn't tell us when the grand human story will come to its unique climax in the return of Christ and the establishing of the kingdom of heaven. The times and seasons are not our business. Being ready and getting the world ready for the King are our business.

Spend a few moments considering your fears for the future. Then spend time considering your hopes for the future. End with prayer, asking God to prepare you to walk confidently and boldly into a future you will help determine.

Matt 25, 31

Last Judgment

(Justice)

Love
care
believe nurture
love
kingdom

7. *9/19*

The Abandonment of Jesus the Messiah

Matthew 26:1–27:31a

Claim Your Story

What kind of disciple are you? We ask that question all the way through the Gospel of Matthew but especially as we come to this poignant section. Another question also arises: What kind of Lord do you follow? What does Christ expect of you, as demonstrated by his expectations of the first disciples?

What can you learn about human nature from the conduct of the religious leaders, of the Good Friday crowd, and of Pilate? How can you protect yourself from the weakness displayed by the disciples? Since Jesus is our ultimate example, what does he show you about divine strength and purpose? How then can you follow Christ with integrity and effectiveness today?

Enter the Bible Story

Each time I read and reread the Gospel of Matthew, I wonder why the disciples were so slow to hear what Jesus was saying about his destination at Calvary. In repeated instances, under circumstances when the disciples should have been especially sensitive to what was being said, Jesus told them of his coming death and resurrection. He spared no words, noting that he would suffer and die and that it would happen in Jerusalem.

However, as he finished his penetrating teaching about ultimate judgment, he said again that the Passover would occur in two days and that he would be "handed over to be crucified" (26:2).

Our human hearing is only partly a matter of the auditory system by which we receive and distinguish sounds. The more crucial factor in our hearing is some kind of inner discretionary system that filters messages through the prior construct of our expectations. So it is that we hear an insult in a benign phrase or we make a compliment out of someone's casual pleasantry.

The disciples were so sure of what Jesus was going to do that they couldn't seem to hear any statements that contradicted those expectations. As a result, they weren't prepared to deal with the crisis when it came. By contrast, the priests and elders knew exactly what they wanted to do; and they moved steadily and stealthily toward their purposes.

Dramas Unfold While Life Goes On

Meanwhile, life goes on in its seemingly ordinary ways. Jesus and his disciples were invited to eat at the home of a man named Simon. The meal was interrupted by a woman who poured an expensive perfume on Jesus. The disciples saw the act as a waste and an extravagance, but Jesus said that the woman had "done a good thing for me" (26:10) because by her gift she had anointed his body for burial. It is as if Jesus was saying that this unknown, unnamed woman understood what was going on better than the disciples did.

Judas Iscariot ("one of the Twelve," Matthew says, as if to underline that the betrayal is coming from within the inner circle itself) sought out the chief priests to volunteer to lead them to Jesus at a time and setting where they could arrest him without fear of the crowds. In this little sequence of events, we see the dullness of the disciples as a whole, the particular betrayal by Judas, the routine hosting by Simon (as if no drama were unfolding), the strange prescience of the anointing woman, and the careful maneuvering of the religious leaders.

Jesus and the disciples then met for the Passover meal. Early in the proceedings Jesus declared that one of them would betray him. It is significant that each one asked if he were the one, a strange question for a select group of loyalists to ask. When Judas asked, Jesus' enigmatic answer let the betrayer know that his plans were no secret to Jesus.

About the Christian Faith

The Eucharist

The Eucharist, derived from the Greek word for "giving thanks" (also known as Communion, the Lord's Supper, the Holy Supper, or the Mass) has traditionally been at the center of Christian worship. It is based upon the final meal of Jesus with his disciples before the Crucifixion, reported in Matthew 26:26-30; Mark 14:22-25; Luke 22:14-20; and 1 Corinthians 11:23-25, each report with a particular nuance.

Weekly celebration of the Eucharist was the pattern in the early church, first as a full meal, then with the bread and wine alone as a symbol or remembrance of the Resurrection. In the early Middle Ages, the Eucharist took on a more somber tone, which lasted until the twentieth century, focusing on Good Friday and the cross. As part of the liturgical renewal movement of the twentieth century, many churches recovered the celebratory character of the Eucharist, again focusing on the Resurrection instead of the cross.

From the ninth century to the present day, there have been different and often competing understandings of exactly how Christ is present in the Eucharist. Despite theological disagreements about the particulars, the church has always affirmed the Eucharist as central to Christian worship.

Jesus broke into the orderly ritual of the Passover meal with what must have seemed a bizarre interval. We miss some of the drama because for us the event is simply the instituting of a sacrament celebrated in one form or another by almost every Christian body, Holy Communion. However, what did the disciples think when Jesus broke bread, told them it was his body, and that they should eat it. What did they think when he took a cup of wine, blessed it, and told them to drink it as his blood?

There was a "perpetual statute throughout your generations," the Torah said, that they should not eat any blood (Leviticus 3:17). Apparently the disciples followed Jesus' instructions without raising any question about the apparent violation, at least symbolically, of their ancient and revered law.

The little gathering sang a hymn and headed to the Mount of Olives. As they did, Jesus confided that all of them would fall away from him but that after his resurrection he would go before them into Galilee. Peter stoutly declared that he would not fail his Lord, not even if he had to die for him. The other disciples echoed Peter's declaration.

From Gethsemane to the Judgment Hall

Nevertheless the process of denial began soon thereafter, in a subtle way, in their inability to support Jesus with prayer during his darkest hour. Jesus led the group to Gethsemane to the place of prayer and asked Peter, James, and John if they would watch with him. Jesus said, "I'm very sad. It's as if I'm dying" (26:38).

The word is well-chosen. The Crucifixion began for Jesus as he prayed in Gethsemane, asking if even yet the cup of suffering might be taken from him: "Not what I want but what you want" (26:39). At this point, Calvary was settled. From here on, the humiliation and suffering, terrible as they were, were postlude.

However, Peter, James, and John fell asleep. Being awakened, they fell asleep again. At the third awakening, Jesus announced that the time had come for his betrayal. While he was still speaking, Judas came with the crowd of priests and elders, carrying swords and clubs. One of the disciples tried to rise to Jesus' defense by striking the high priest's slave with his sword, but Jesus rebuked the effort. If he wanted to do so, Jesus said, he could call "twelve battle groups of angels" to his defense. However, to do so would violate the purposes of Scripture (26:53-54).

At this point, "all the disciples left Jesus and ran away" (26:56). I sense that their fleeing was caused as much by their bewilderment as by cowardice or fear. They simply couldn't understand what was happening to Jesus or why he would surrender to the enemy if it were in his power to resist.

To Peter's credit, he stayed close enough "to see how it would turn out" (26:58). The chief priests and the council had become desperate enough in their desire to be done with Jesus that they solicited false testimony with which to put him to death, but without success. Then two witnesses recalled Jesus saying, "I can destroy God's temple and rebuild it in three days" (26:61), a somewhat misshapen recollection of Jesus' reference to the destruction and resurrection of his own body.

Throughout the questions and accusations, Jesus remained silent, until the high priest demanded, "Tell us whether you are the Christ, God's Son," to which Jesus replied, "You have said so. But I tell you,

From now on you will see the Son of Man / seated at the right hand of Power / and coming on the clouds of heaven" (26:64, New Revised Standard Version).

With this, the high priest "tore his clothes" and asked rhetorically, "Why do we need any more witnesses?" The high priest was right. Jesus had made a claim for himself that justified the charges that were being brought against him. The high priest's statement unleashed the venom that was pent up against Jesus. Although the power of execution was reserved only for the Roman government, members of the council— scholars, public leaders, and men of honor—spat in Jesus' face, beat him, and mocked him in a style that would have embarrassed raucous schoolboys. Peter watched it all. Later, he denied his Lord three times before fleeing the scene.

By now it was early in the morning. They bound Jesus and brought him to Pilate, the governor and the ranking authority of Rome in that area. Judas, the betrayer, seeing that Jesus would be put to death, "felt deep regret" (27:3). Apparently, like Simon Peter, Judas had been watching the trial from a distance. There is some irony in the fact that the two disciples who are reported as seeing what was happening included one who denied his Lord and the other who betrayed him.

Judas tried to make it right. He confessed to the chief priests and elders that he had "betrayed an innocent man." They replied, "What is that to us? That's your problem" (27:4). Their answer was true, of course. There is a point in our relationship to God and in the unfolding of our conduct when the issue is ours alone. Others may have influenced us, but the final decisions are ours.

The question for Judas was how he would proceed. Would he find his way through the sullen mob until he could get near enough to Jesus to be heard so that he could call out his repentance to the one he had betrayed? Instead, futilely, Judas threw down the silver pieces he had been paid and went out and hanged himself.

While the chief priests and elders were theologically correct in telling Judas that he would have to be responsible for his own conduct, it was equally true that they had to be responsible for theirs. When Judas tried to withdraw his action, declaring that he had betrayed an innocent man,

Across the Testaments

Matthew and the Hebrew Scriptures

Citation in Matthew	Old Testament Reference
Matthew 26:2, 17 Passover	*Exodus 12–13* An annual festival to celebrate liberation from Egypt.
Matthew 26:6-7 A woman anoints Jesus with expensive perfume.	*Exodus 29:7; Leviticus 21:10* Anointing of priests *1 Samuel 10:1; 2 Kings 9:3, 6* Anointing of kings
Matthew 26:28 Jesus offers the cup to his disciples.	*Exodus 24:8* Moses sprinkles the blood of the covenant of the Lord. *Jeremiah 31:31-34* Promise of a new covenant
Matthew 26:31, 56 Jesus cites Zechariah 13:7, foreseeing that the disciples will desert him.	*Zechariah 13:7* "Strike the shepherd, that the sheep may be scattered" (NRSV).
Matthew 26:64 Jesus cites Daniel 7:13-14.	*Daniel 7:13-14* A vision of the coming of the Son of Man
Matthew 27:9-10 Matthew names Jeremiah but actually cites Zechariah 11:12-13.	*Zechariah 11:12-13* Thirty shekels of silver

an ethical weight fell upon the priests and elders. If their informant said he had erred, then they should have reexamined the action they had taken with his assistance.

However, instead of using Judas's confession as a basis for self-examination and reconsideration, the religious leaders directed their attention to a less important but more convenient matter of their law: how to use the betrayal money that had been returned to them. With scrupulous religiosity, they dedicated the thirty pieces of silver to purchase a potter's field, a burial place for strangers. They put bad money to a good end. One wonders how frequently this is done in our day.

Pilate: The Politician and the Man

When Jesus was brought before Pilate, he made no attempt to defend himself. He remained silent as accusations were made. Even at our guiltiest moments, most of us offer a word of explanation or an appeal for understanding or mercy. Jesus "didn't answer, not even a single word." No wonder Pilate "was greatly amazed" (27:14).

He did, however, draw conclusions. Pilate was no fool. He sensed that something out of the ordinary was unfolding in his otherwise-routine place of judgment. He must have seen the flimsy quality of the case the priests and elders were bringing. He must also have seen qualities in Jesus—even in his battered and humiliated state—that impressed him. Pilate must have been intrigued by Jesus' indifference to the charges being brought against him and the peace and even the sense of purpose Jesus demonstrated at the prospect of death, a terrifying method of death at that.

Experienced as he was in the art of political compromise, Pilate offered a counter plan. As governor, on a feast day he could release to the crowd a prisoner of their choosing. He had a good foil. A "well-known prisoner named Jesus Barabbas" was in custody (27:16). He offered the crowd a choice between "Jesus Barabbas or Jesus who is called Christ" (27:17).

The plan was that of a master politician. The decision was put into the hands of the crowd. It seemed to Pilate that it could hardly go wrong: The crowd would surely choose the healer and teacher called Jesus Christ over the "well-known prisoner" Barabbas.

If the crowds chose Jesus, it was significant that Pilate described him not by the conventional style of the time, which would have been Jesus of Nazareth, but by the name Pilate knew offended the religious leaders: "who is called Christ," that is, the Messiah. If the crowds chose Jesus the Christ, it would be a declaration that they saw him as their Messiah; and it would be a humiliating rebuke to the chief priests and elders.

However, the chief priests and elders were better than average politicians in their own right. They hadn't gotten to their positions by careless errors. They understood crowds and how easily a crowd can mount to irrational fervor. The crowd didn't disappoint them. They called for Barabbas to be released and for Jesus to be crucified.

Meanwhile, Pilate's soul had heard another voice. It didn't have the volume of the crowd or the political influence of the chief priests and elders, but it was louder than either one. His wife sent a message: "Leave that righteous man alone. I've suffered much today in a dream because of him" (27:19).

We don't know what kind of woman Pilate's wife was. Obviously she was accustomed to the world of political and economic power. She knew the benefits and the perils of public office; but somewhere in her soul there was a sensitivity to God, to morality, to justice, a doorway through which her conscience could speak to her in a dream.

Without a doubt, Pilate was moved by what he had seen of Jesus (and by contrast, of Jesus' accusers) and by what he had heard from his wife. When the crowd had their choice, they called for Barabbas to be released and for Christ to be crucified. When Pilate tried to reason with the crowd (a futile effort, of course, because a crowd is not a reasoning creature) by asking, "Why? What wrong has he done?" the shouts of the crowd grew even louder. "Crucify him" (27:23).

So Pilate did what he has been remembered for doing ever since. He took water and washed his hands. "I'm innocent of this man's blood," he said. "It's your problem" (27:24). However, ultimately none of us can eliminate ourselves from our moral responsibilities. Surely no one can excuse himself or herself from the challenge that Christ inevitably presents to all who meet him.

You discover how inescapable the Christ judgment is when you see what follows. The crowd accepted its responsibility for Jesus' crucifixion, and Pilate released Barabbas. Then Pilate "had Jesus whipped" before handing him over for crucifixion. Why the whipping? Why did Pilate choose personally to humiliate Jesus and to add to his pain? After all, there was no reason why Pilate should step down from the dignity of his office to an act of base cruelty.

Was it because he was angry with Jesus for the problems Jesus had unintentionally brought to him; or was he trying to tell the religious leaders and the crowd that he, too, thought Jesus ought to suffer? Was Pilate so angry with his inability to deal with good and evil that he took out his feelings of moral inadequacy on the innocent one?

After the whipping, Pilate handed Jesus over to the soldiers. A whole company of soldiers (perhaps six hundred of them) gathered around, stripped Jesus, and then robed him in a garment of mock authority. They also made him wear a crown of thorns and carry a stick that looked like a ridiculous scepter. With that, they made a great show of bowing before Jesus, addressing him as king of the Jews, and stopping at times to spit on him.

One wonders what makes humans treat anyone so inhumanely, and then one realizes that it is because we are capable of such cruelty that we need a Savior. The voices of the condemning crowd, the cheap political maneuvering of the chief priests and elders, and the baseless cruelty of Pilate and the soldiers led seamlessly to Calvary. The price of sin is high; we need a Savior.

Live the Story

How do you respond to this portion of Jesus' story? Looking at an event two millennia old, we'd like to distance ourselves from the conduct of our human ancestors. However, we can't honestly say that people were more brutal in those days, in light of the violence that sells so many movies and video games in our day.

Our personal uneasiness with the story increases when we remember how even Jesus' chosen followers forsook him at the time of greatest need. This—and also on the basis of the disciples' failure—should cause us to recognize our human frailty and to fortify ourselves for our own times of testing. What kind of disciple are you when facing troubling, challenging, even frightening situations?

Clearly, our best example is in our Lord. We see how he struggled in Gethsemane to recommit himself to the will of God, regardless of the price. Deep within we know that this is the ultimate hope of our planet: that those who take the name of Christ will follow him in seeking for and living out the will of God in our needy world.

Taking as long as you like, meditate upon Jesus Christ in the garden of Gethsemane with yourself next to him in prayer. How willing are you to earnestly seek the will of God and what are you willing to sacrifice in order to live out the will of God in our needy world?

8.

The Death and Resurrection of Jesus

Matthew 27:31b–28:20

Claim Your Story

You are coming to the end of Matthew's report. The few pages in which the story concludes are packed with shame, pain, mystery, power, and wonder.

So what does it mean to you nearly twenty centuries later? What does it tell you about Jesus and his role in your story? What significance for you is there in the long-ago death of a wandering teacher who was brought to trial and executed and was reported to have been raised from the dead on the third day after his execution? Does this matter today? What difference does it make to your living and dying?

What does it tell you about the nature of God? What do you know about God that you wouldn't know if Jesus' death and resurrection hadn't happened?

What difference does it make that Jesus of Nazareth, the Christ, carried a cross to a hill outside Jerusalem, died in humiliation and rejection, and then rose again? Should you live differently today because this happened? Does Jesus' death and resurrection place any responsibility or call upon you?

Enter the Bible Story

We don't know what brought a man from Cyrene named Simon to Jerusalem at this time. Perhaps it was a typical business trip, or perhaps he had come to celebrate the Passover. In any event, he was conscripted from the role of a bystander to become an unforgettable supporting actor, carrying Jesus' cross the last tortuous distance to Golgotha. Matthew reminds us that the name of the hill meant "skull place." The place in contemporary Jerusalem shown to tourists still has the appearance of a human skull, which may explain its name. Some feel the name came from the human skeletons that accumulated there from the crucifixions.

Jesus' crucifixion was simply another day at work for the Roman soldiers. There was a side benefit, however. The soldiers inherited the clothing of the victims. So the soldiers divided Jesus' possessions—the clothes he wore—without the aid of court or of trust officers. Two other men were crucified with Jesus, to his right and left. They are described simply as "two thieves"; no distinctive crimes are named, just common criminals of the daily lot.

However, the thieves must have wondered about the man between them when they saw those who came to mock him, elegantly dressed community leaders, men who carried themselves with the confidence of their office. They were chief priest, legal experts, and elders of the people.

As they came near Jesus' cross, these men of dignity and position suddenly became coarse beyond description, mocking Jesus by quoting sentences from their dialogues with him. "He saved others, but he can't save himself. . . . He trusts in God, so let God deliver him now if he wants to" (27:42-43). Emboldened by these attacks, the two thieves joined in the slander. They had never before been able to offer their opinions in such distinguished company and were surprised to find that they fit in so comfortably with people of apparent authority.

Jesus Cries Out in a Loud Voice

Matthew gives us a physical detail that he found significant: "From noon until three in the afternoon the whole earth was dark" (27:45). For centuries, Christians have celebrated these hours of darkness in *Tre Ore* services of solemn worship and remembrance. For Matthew, obviously, the physical phenomenon was evidence that nature itself was grieving. The voice that had called them into existence was now being silenced.

At about three o'clock, Jesus spoke words that are described as his cry of abandonment: "My God, my God, why have you left me?"(27:46). Jesus was quoting the opening words of Psalm 22.

Because in Hebrew the first words sound like the name of the prophet Elijah—and no doubt because Elijah was associated in their teaching with the Messiah—some bystanders said, "He's calling Elijah." One sensitive soul ran with a sponge of vinegar to ease Jesus' pain; but the others said, "Let's see if Elijah will come and save him" (27:49). Now Jesus "cried out with a loud shout." Clearly, this was no dying gasp, no last exhaling. It was a declaration of finality, of achievement, an announcement of life's work done.

Again, Matthew reports an extraordinary sidebar: "The curtain of the sanctuary was torn in two from top to bottom. The earth shook, the rocks split, and the bodies of many holy people who had died were raised" (27:51-52). The Temple curtain to which Matthew refers was described by Josephus as being sixty feet high. It separated the holy place from the most holy. Some feel that its being torn represented the judgment of God on the Jewish religious leaders. At the least, it demonstrated that the way to God was now opened in a fashion never known before. When Matthew speaks of the resurrection of many "holy people," he no doubt is letting his readers know that the power of death has now been made absurd through the death of Jesus Christ.

A centurion, a trusted military leader from Rome, said, "This was certainly God's Son" (27:54). Some scholars feel that this centurion, who no doubt believed in multiple gods, was simply putting Jesus in that category. Others believe that he was making a unique declaration for our Lord. Obviously no one can speak finally as to what was going on in the mind and soul of the centurion. In any event, most conversions are of several parts, from less belief to more convinced and productive belief. I welcome the centurion at whatever was the juncture in his holy journey.

We remember that on the night of Jesus' arrest, his disciples forsook him and fled. Now Matthew says, "Many women were watching from a distance. They had followed Jesus from Galilee to serve him" (27:55). Count these women as the founders of every Catholic and Orthodox order

Across the Testaments

Matthew and the Hebrew Scriptures

Citation in Matthew	Old Testament Reference
Matthew 27:35 Roman soldiers cast lots for Jesus' clothes.	*Psalm 22:18* Enemies of the psalmist claim his clothes.
Matthew 27:46 Jesus quotes Psalm 22:1.	*Psalm 22:1* "My God, my God, why have you forsaken me?" (NRSV).
Matthew 27:51-53 The curtain of the Temple is torn in two.	*Exodus 26:31-35; 40:21* The curtain of the Tabernacle

of nuns and every Protestant organization of deaconesses and parish workers. They had sought to serve Jesus in every way they could within a culture that allowed them little opportunity for leadership. Now they were with him still, staying as close as possible. It seems clear that they were hoping to serve him still, even in his death.

Probably tens of thousands of persons died by crucifixion in the roughly six centuries that it was practiced as a form of execution prior to the death of Jesus. The Roman government used crucifixion as a means of controlling crime and possible insurrection. On occasions, hundreds were crucified at one time. How is it, then, that the crucifixion of Jesus has become singularly significant?

Quite directly because from the beginning the church has understood that the death of Jesus was not simply an act by the Roman government or the end of a plot set up by Jesus' enemies. Rather, it was God's action against sin and death.

The earliest writings of the New Testament, the epistles, make the Crucifixion central. The Book of Hebrews carefully ties it to events and figures in the Hebrew Scriptures. The four Gospels give a disproportionate amount of their pages to this single event, sometimes to the neglect of other matters we wish they might have emphasized. The Book of Revelation gives startling prominence to Jesus as the slain Lamb of God, the only one worthy to open heaven's books.

God Suffers With Jesus

We will never understand the Crucifixion unless we see the power, the repugnance, and the unceasing threat of sin. Nor will we understand it until we realize the profound quality of God's love for our human race. We will misinterpret the cross if we see it as God's action on Christ.

Rather, the cross is a Trinitarian event: God suffers with Christ at Calvary, and the Holy Spirit is the voice of this pain. When Christ cries, "My God, my God, why have you left me?" (27:46), it is the cry of a rupture within the heart of God. As such, it is God's action against sin and the ultimate expression of God's love for our human race and his creation.

Returning to the Crucifixion scene, we see another unlikely figure entering the drama. Earlier, Simon the Cyrenian came into the story through no thought of his own, snatched from the crowd like a divine lottery chance. However, now another stranger, Joseph of Arimathea, enters the story by deliberate and hazardous choice.

Previously a secret disciple, Joseph now came forward to ask Pilate for Jesus' body. Because he was a man of property and position, his request was granted. I suspect Pilate wondered why a man of Joseph's standing would involve himself with Jesus. Perhaps it even pricked Pilate's conscience that Joseph would affiliate himself with Jesus when Pilate would not.

Joseph wanted permission to take Jesus' body for an honorable burial. He wrapped it in traditional clean linen, laid it in his own new tomb, rolled a large stone to the door of the tomb, and went away. "Mary Magdalene and the other Mary were there, sitting in front of the tomb" (27:61).

An unnerving thought now occurred to the chief priests and Pharisees. They remembered that Jesus had said that after three days he would arise. What if his disciples should come and steal the body? They appealed to Pilate for help, and Pilate responded with full empowerment:

"Make it as secure as you know how" (27:65). So they sealed the stone and posted the guard.

The Empty Tomb

The sabbath passed, Matthew tells us, and Mary Magdalene and the other Mary came "at dawn on the first day of the week" (28:1). Call it, indeed, the first day of a new world. If ever a dawn has broken for the human race, it was on this day when lonely, loving women came to fulfill what they felt would be their last measurable act of devotion to their Lord.

One wonders what the women said as they made this unique journey. We assume that previously they had expected, as did the Twelve, that Jesus would set up Israel's new kingdom. After all, he had preached and taught the Kingdom message from the beginning. It seems likely that their motives were a step better than that of the disciples because they held no dream of being at Jesus' right hand and left, as did James and John and other disciples. It was a world where women held little prospect of political preferment. I suspect they hoped simply to serve him in any way possible.

Now the only service remaining was to place with his body the traditional memorial spices and perfumes. Watch well these women and Joseph of Arimathea. Their dreams may have been crushed, but their love and devotion were as great as ever.

Somewhere between the darkness and the dawn, on that momentous third day, "an angel from the Lord came down from heaven. Coming to the stone, he rolled it away and sat on it" (28:2). This angel is described in the kind of language one will find later in the Book of Revelation: dramatic, extravagant, out-of-this-world. However, like virtually every other biblical messenger, this angel reassures by saying, "Don't be afraid" (28:5). He knew why they had come; and he reminded them of what they had been told earlier: that Jesus would be raised from the dead. Now he was already on the way to Galilee.

Matthew tells us that they moved with "great fear and excitement" (28:8). I should think so! They had not gone far when Jesus himself greeted them. He, too, told them not to be afraid. It's interesting that Jesus' birth and resurrection brought fear and then reassurance against the fear. I suspect that if we begin to comprehend God's action in our world in Jesus' coming and his resurrection, we will properly be struck with awe.

How is it that the eternal God would visit our planet in such a personal and redemptive way? What is it that makes us human creatures of such value?

Matthew interrupts his account at this point to report on another frantic attempt by the chief priests and elders to deal with a situation that is obviously out of their control. For a moment the drama of resurrection has this comedy sequence: Men of intentional dignity—dressed to their role as intellectual, religious, and political leaders—turned their frantic attention to an absurd, schoolboy plot to bribe a group of soldiers. "So the soldiers took the money and did as they were told" (28:15).

I smile as I observe the glee of the guards. They had expected, no doubt, that they would lose their work if not their lives for letting a corpse escape. Instead they received a huge bonus! Yes, it is a bit of divine comedy relief.

The next sentence, however, is one of pathos. "Now the eleven disciples went to Galilee" (28:16). The apostolic census is sad. The disciples had numbered twelve. As faithful Jews, they understood in at least a measure that their number was like that of the twelve tribes of Israel. However, one of their group had defected, and now there were eleven. Mind you, all of them had at one point fled from Jesus, but these eleven had been able to rejoin their Lord and be restored to ministry. Judas, however, was gone.

So they came to a mountain. Our journey with the disciples, under Matthew's guidance, began for all significant purposes at a mountain where Jesus outlined the wonders and demands of his Kingdom (Matthew 5–7). Now it was a mountain again as they entered the new world of the Resurrection.

Centuries removed, as you and I are, we expect that these eleven men will be of one mind and passion; but we weren't there. If we had been, our feelings would have been more divided. So Matthew tells us candidly, "When they saw him, they worshipped him, but some doubted" (28:17).

I am unceasingly grateful for the honesty of the Scriptures. The Scriptures are not a public relations document nor are they a defense of the faith. They are an unvarnished report of what happened, with all the human elements of faith and failure, wonder and doubt, left intact.

Jesus Commissions His Followers

Jesus proceeded to reassure his followers and to challenge them. "I've received all authority in heaven and on earth" (28:18). There was no equivocating or modifying in this declaration. *All* is inclusive; and in case his followers might wonder the extent of the reach of *all*, Jesus made it clear: "in heaven and on earth." He, the crucified and resurrected one, now defines the extent of the Kingdom he has proclaimed from the beginning. He assures his followers that his authority extends over it all.

Without a pause, Jesus told his followers what this meant to them. It was not something to sit back and enjoy, nor was it about finding a seat at Jesus' right or left. "Therefore, go and make disciples of all nations, baptizing them in the name of the Father and of the Son and of the Holy Spirit, teaching them to obey everything that I've commanded you" (28:19-20). Jesus' disciples are to go and make other disciples. They are to do so without sense of national and ethnic boundaries ("all nations"), and thus their job is not done until all nations are reached. They are given a structure for decision: Those who follow will receive baptism. For the first time, the Trinitarian formula—Father, Son, and Holy Spirit—is spelled out specifically and clearly.

We are not only to be evangelists to the nations, seeking their baptism, but we are to be teachers. If evangelism is to move beyond converts to disciples, it will need to instruct its converts carefully and fully so they know what their Lord expects of them.

Now all of this is surely a daunting assignment. Perhaps some of the disciples sensed such a possibility when they looked at Jesus and doubted, because the fear of a teacher's assignments often makes us wonder if we've signed up for the course we want to follow. Jesus offered a word of ultimate reassurance: "Look, I myself will be with you every day until the end of this present age" (28:20).

Personally, I can't imagine a more satisfying, more thrilling, more demanding word. I like Matthew's conclusion!

Live the Story

You have come to the end of Matthew's report; but for you it is, as it was for the disciples, the beginning. This is not a story to be read and enjoyed and then laid aside. Nor is it a story simply to be discussed and speculated upon. For those who will receive it, that is, for those who accept its message and become disciples, Matthew's record is a compelling call.

You have learned of one who came to declare the kingdom of heaven. You have followed his story to the place of death, the place where he delivered himself in the person of God to break the power of sin and death. Then you have followed him from the place of resurrection to another mountain, where he calls you to carry his love and redemption to all the world.

Now the burden and the wonder, the truth and the challenge, are yours! In some way, share with another the joy that death could not hold Jesus Christ in the grave.

Leader Guide

People often view the Bible as a maze of obscure people, places, and events from centuries ago and struggle to relate it to their daily lives. IMMERSION invites us to experience the Bible as a record of God's loving revelation to humankind. These studies recognize our emotional, spiritual, and intellectual needs and welcome us into the Bible story and into deeper faith.

As leader of an IMMERSION group, you will help participants to encounter the Word of God and the God of the Word that will lead to new creation in Christ. You do not have to be an expert to lead; in fact, you will participate with your group in listening to and applying God's life-transforming Word to your lives. You and your group will explore the building blocks of the Christian faith through key stories, people, ideas, and teachings in every book of the Bible. You will also explore the bridges and points of connection between the Old and New Testaments.

Choosing and Using the Bible

The central goal of IMMERSION is engaging the members of your group with the Bible in a way that informs their minds, forms their hearts, and transforms the way they live out their Christian faith. Participants will need this study book and a Bible. IMMERSION is an excellent accompaniment to the Common English Bible (CEB). It shares with the CEB four common aims: clarity of language, faith in the Bible's power to transform lives, the emotional expectation that people will find the love of God, and the rational expectation that people will find the knowledge of God.

Other recommended study Bibles include *The New Interpreter's Study Bible* (NRSV), *The New Oxford Annotated Study Bible* (NRSV), *The HarperCollins Study Bible* (NRSV), the *NIV and TNIV Study Bibles*, and the *Archaeological Study Bible* (NIV). Encourage participants to use more than one translation. *The Message: The Bible in Contemporary Language* is a modern paraphrase of the Bible, based on the original languages. Eugene H. Peterson has created a masterful presentation of the Scripture text, which is best used alongside rather than in place of the CEB or another primary English translation.

One of the most reliable interpreters of the Bible's meaning is the Bible itself. Invite participants first of all to allow Scripture to have its say. Pay attention to context. Ask questions of the text. Read every passage with curiosity, always seeking to answer the basic Who? What? Where? When? and Why? questions.

Bible study groups should also have handy essential reference resources in case someone wants more information or needs clarification on specific words, terms, concepts, places, or people mentioned in the Bible. A Bible dictionary, Bible atlas, concordance, and one-volume Bible commentary together make for a good, basic reference library.

The Leader's Role

An effective leader prepares ahead. This leader guide provides easy to follow, step-by-step suggestions for leading a group. The key task of the leader is to guide discussion and activities that will engage heart and head and will invite faith development. Discussion questions are included, and you may want to add questions posed by you or your group. Here are suggestions for helping your group engage Scripture:

State questions clearly and simply.

Ask questions that move Bible truths from "outside" (dealing with concepts, ideas, or information about a passage) to "inside" (relating to the experiences, hopes, and dreams of the participants).

Work for variety in your questions, including compare and contrast, information recall, motivation, connections, speculation, and evaluation.

Avoid questions that call for yes-or-no responses or answers that are obvious.

Don't be afraid of silence during a discussion. It often yields especially thoughtful comments.

Test questions before using them by attempting to answer them yourself.

When leading a discussion, pay attention to the mood of your group by "listening" with your eyes as well as your ears.

Guidelines for the Group

IMMERSION is designed to promote full engagement with the Bible for the purpose of growing faith and building up Christian community. While much can be gained from individual reading, a group Bible study offers an ideal setting in which to achieve these aims. Encourage participants to bring their Bibles and read from Scripture during the session. Invite participants to consider the following guidelines as they participate in the group:

Respect differences of interpretation and understanding.

Support one another with Christian kindness, compassion, and courtesy.

Listen to others with the goal of understanding rather than agreeing or disagreeing.

Celebrate the opportunity to grow in faith through Bible study.

Approach the Bible as a dialogue partner, open to the possibility of being challenged or changed by God's Word.

Recognize that each person brings unique and valuable life experiences to the group and is an important part of the community.

Reflect theologically—that is, be attentive to three basic questions: What does this say about God? What does this say about me/us? What does this say about the relationship between God and me/us?

Commit to a *lived faith response* in light of insights you gain from the Bible. In other words, what changes in attitudes (how you believe) or actions (how you behave) are called for by God's Word?

Group Sessions

The group sessions, like the chapters themselves, are built around three sections: "Claim Your Story," "Enter the Bible Story," and "Live the Story." Sessions are designed to move participants from an awareness of their own life story, issues, needs, and experiences into an encounter and dialogue with the story of Scripture and to make decisions integrating their personal stories and the Bible's story.

The session plans in the following pages will provide questions and activities to help your group focus on the particular content of each chapter. In addition to questions and activities, the plans will include chapter title, Scripture, and faith focus.

Here are things to keep in mind for all the sessions:

Prepare Ahead

Study the Scripture, comparing different translations and perhaps a paraphrase.
Read the chapter, and consider what it says about your life and the Scripture.
Gather materials such as large sheets of paper or a markerboard with markers.
Prepare the learning area. Write the faith focus for all to see.

Welcome Participants

Invite participants to greet one another.
Tell them to find one or two people and talk about the faith focus.
Ask: What words stand out for you? Why?

Guide the Session

Look together at "Claim Your Story." Ask participants to give their reactions to the stories and examples given in each chapter. Use questions from the session plan to elicit comments based on personal experiences and insights.

Ask participants to open their Bibles and "Enter the Bible Story." For each portion of Scripture, use questions from the session plan to help participants gain insight into the text and relate it to issues in their lives.

Step through the activity or questions posed in "Live the Story." Encourage participants to embrace what they have learned and apply it in their daily lives.

Invite participants to offer their responses or insights about the boxed material in "Across the Testaments," "About the Scripture," and "About the Christian Faith."

Close the Session

Encourage participants to read the following week's Scripture and chapter before the next session.
Offer a closing prayer.

1. The Birth of Jesus
Matthew 1–2

Faith Focus
Just as particular persons chose to cooperate with God's purposes surrounding the birth of Jesus, we too can choose to be instruments of God's grace.

Before the Session
After reading the birth story in Matthew 1–2, take time to compare it with the birth narratives found in Luke and Mark. Pay attention to which details the Gospel writers include in their respective accounts. Also, consider bringing to the group session a full Nativity set, placing it in a central location in the room for people to view and possibly pass around during the opening discussion.

Claim Your Story
Invite participants to share their earliest memories of seeing a Christmas pageant that depicted the story of Jesus' birth, hearing the story read aloud from a Bible storybook, or discussing the story while positioning the figures of a Nativity set. Talk together about what each person believes is the most meaningful or significant aspect of Jesus' birth story.

Why do you think the three Gospel writers—Matthew, Mark, and Luke—each chose to tell the story of Jesus' birth in a particular way? What does Matthew's version say to you about what he thought was the most important aspect of Jesus' birth?

What does our culture's celebration of Christmas say about how people understand Jesus' birth? What does your church's observance of Christmas say about how your congregation understands Jesus' birth?

Enter the Bible Story
Matthew 1
Point out that in the ancient world, being able to trace your family pedigree was of utmost significance. Past ancestry was an indicator of present character and future promise. For Matthew, Jesus is part of Jewish history as well as the breaking point in the history of all people.

Because of Matthew's special emphasis on Jewish history, a box has been included with each session called "Matthew and the Hebrew Scriptures," giving examples of Matthew passages that echo Old Testament Scripture. Such boxes will be found throughout the *Immersion* studies, to offer extra information and insight. Essentially, what Matthew does in Chapter 1 is shout that Jesus is what the world has been waiting for.

What does it say to you about God that Jesus, our Redeemer, was sent into the world through a lineage that included scandalous, even sinful, ancestors?

In Matthews' birth drama (1:18-24), the angel's first instruction to Joseph was "Don't be afraid." When have you found yourself afraid to follow through on something you weren't sure was in God's plan? How did God's assurance come to you?

Matthew's story mentions two names for the Christ Child: *Jesus* ("Because he will save his people from their sins," 1:21) and *Emmanuel* ("which means, 'God with us,'" 1:25). Which name carries the most meaning for you? Why?

Matthew 2

As with any good story, Matthew's Nativity story features a "bad guy": King Herod. In this second chapter, pay attention to the contrasting motivations and actions of the bad guy, Herod, and the good guys, the magi.

What about Jesus' coming most frightened King Herod? What about the coming of Jesus into your life makes you (or has made you) afraid?

The magi went looking for a new king; instead they found a child. Apparently they made a leap of faith when they bowed down in worship of a king who did not meet their expectations. What about Jesus calls for you to make a leap of faith to trust in who he is? What change of direction or priorities has your faith in Jesus challenged you to make?

Live the Story

Go around the group and say what would be missing if you didn't know the Christmas story as Matthew tells it, establishing Jesus' roots in the history of Israel and in the Hebrew Scriptures. What would you be missing if you did not know the particular names in Jesus' family tree, especially the women? What would you be missing if you didn't know about Joseph's special role in the story? What would you be missing if Matthew hadn't mentioned the magi, learned visitors from a land far beyond Israel's borders? What would you be missing if all you knew was the happy domesticated Christmas story expressed in greeting cards?

What does Mathew's account of Jesus' birth suggest to you about the way God works in the world and in your life? What does it suggest about how God might use a person like you in being a witness to the continuing story of Jesus Christ?

Invite each person to take a folded piece of paper the size of a standard Christmas card and write out or draw a simple message proclaiming a truth related to the story of Jesus' birth. The message should reflect the person's response to the question: What does Jesus' birth mean for your life?

2. Jesus' Identity Is Confirmed and Tested
Matthew 3–4

Faith Focus
Confirmed by God and confronted by worldly temptation, Jesus models for us faithful obedience by remaining true to himself and his mission.

Before the Session
The accounts of Jesus' baptism and temptation concern the crucial issue of his identity as the One sent by God to proclaim good news. Matthew wants to establish who Jesus is before telling about what Jesus does. Consider why that is important. You may want to have your group discuss how the ritual of baptism and experiences of temptation in life affect Christian witness. Also note that John the Baptist and Jesus utter the same proclamation: "Repent, for the kingdom of heaven has come near" (3:2; 4:17). What do you think that repetition signals?

Claim Your Story
Show the group a Bible given at baptism or a photo taken immediately following a baptism. Ask those in the group who have been baptized to give a brief account of their experience. For those who were not baptized or who don't remember their baptism, go around the group and hear brief accounts of people's baptisms. Some may have no memory of that experience. In those cases, invite them to share a meaningful experience of witnessing a baptism. Once everyone has had a chance to speak, discuss these questions:

What does your baptism mean to you now?

To whom or what does your baptism connect you/us?

Invite the group to reflect silently on their memories of facing temptations or trials in life. After a minute or so, discuss these questions:

Why do you think you sometimes give in to temptation? What trials do you find threatening, and why?

What connection do you see between the particular temptations or trials you face and the trust you have in God's claim on your life?

Enter the Bible Story
Matthew 3
The Common English Bible translates the Greek word *metanoeite* in Matthew 3:2 with the phrase "change your hearts and lives," while other versions translate the word as "repent." The emphasis is correctly on change, for in the beginning of Matthew's Gospel, John the Baptist and Jesus are calling for radical change; and that change involves an act: the ritual of baptism.

Why are John and Jesus calling for change? Change *from* what? Change *for* what?

How does Jesus' baptism symbolize or signify the change he and John were calling for?

In what ways did your baptism prepare you for or set you on a path of a changed life? What does it say about Jesus that he willingly submitted to John's baptism along with others?

Matthew 4

In reading the temptation story, keep in mind key points made in your book. First, the flip side of Satan's base temptations are God's high expectations. Jesus chose not the easy way or the shortcut, but God's way. Second, legitimate needs or desires are most often the entry points for temptation. Jesus' hunger was no different from any creature's hunger, yet he recognized that more was at stake than simply a full stomach.

Why do you think Satan begins his first two tests by addressing Jesus as the Son of God?

Jesus' three temptations concern *entitlement* ("You deserve this so make it so."), *identity* ("You are somebody special so take it."), and *power* ("You can be like God so go for it."). Which of the three issues are, for you, the avenues where temptation most often comes into your life?

The writer states, "We open the door for heavenly visits when we close the door to temptation." When has that been true for you?

Live the Story

Recall that Jesus, whose spirituality was so evident that John was reluctant to baptize him, insisted that he must accept the role of religious ritual—a vigorous challenge to our age of independent spirituality. Considering Jesus' reliance on ritual, spend a few minutes talking together about how the rituals of your church help you connect with God and one another.

Invite participants to be present at the next service of baptism for the purpose of remembering and celebrating their own baptisms and for listening afresh to what God has called them to be as baptized believers. What do the vows require of family and church congregants?

Consider Jesus' wilderness experience. In some ways it is the one incident in Jesus' life that seems most to resonate with our own stories. Challenge each person to choose and memorize three Scripture passages that might be especially helpful for them in withstanding tests and temptations.

3. The Sermon on the Mount
Matthew 5–7

Faith Focus

Jesus invites us to a new orientation to life, an "impossible possibility" that places us within God's new community.

Before the Session

Note that the Sermon on the Mount does not so much present good advice for us to follow but rather proclaims good news about a way of life that his coming has already made possible. What implications might that idea have? Search the Internet for advertisements claiming to promote or increase personal happiness, peace, and contentment. Print a few of these, and make a collage poster out of them. Bring it to the group session to prompt the opening discussion.

Prepare a page with just the Beatitudes text from Matthew 5:3-12, and make copies to give to each participant at the close of your session.

Claim Your Story

Show the poster collage of Internet advertisements, and invite people to comment on the kinds of happiness being promoted. Ask what other advertisements people saw this past week on television, on the Internet, in magazines, or on billboards.

Why do you think our culture promotes the notion that happiness is a byproduct of possessions, prestige, or power?

Why do we, as Christians, often experience unhappiness when we do not have the things our world defines as essential to personal happiness? What can we do about it?

Enter the Bible Story
Matthew 5

The pronouncements that Jesus makes here are invitations to see the new way the world works from God's perspective; and to see that, by following Jesus, we can begin living that way even now. The images of salt and light are vivid descriptions of our potential impact on the world.

What aspects of the Beatitudes seem most inviting to you? Why? Which aspects seem most daunting or disturbing to you? Why?

When have you had an opportunity to act as a light in a dark moment or in the midst of someone else's darkness?

Have you had an experience of "turning the other cheek" or "loving your enemies" as Jesus encourages? What was the result?

Matthew 6
Practical piety and prayer are Jesus' themes here. In addition, he proclaims the uselessness of worldly worries. Consider the connections between the Lord's Prayer (6:9-13) and the Beatitudes (5:3-12).

How do you "practice your piety" in your own life? Where do prayer and fasting or other spiritual disciplines fit into your life, or how could they?

As inviting as it sounds, trying to follow Jesus' command "Do not worry about your life" is difficult for modern Christians. What makes it especially difficult for you? What would it take for you to worry less?

Matthew 7
The linchpin of this chapter is the Golden Rule (7:12). While the gist of it appears in other ancient documents, and often in the negative ("Do not do . . ."), here Jesus casts the truth in a positive way. In everything, he says, act in consideration of the other person. It sounds so easy.

Why do you think following the Golden Rule is so difficult, even for Christians?
In what ways have you tried to build your spiritual house on sand? on rock?

Live the Story
The Sermon on the Mount is like a spiritual Mount Everest: Millions of us recognize its name, but few of us dare to approach its heights. Some of the loveliest declarations in this sermon are also the most challenging.

Ask members of your group to share the parts of Jesus' Sermon on the Mount that challenge or trouble them the most. Make a list of these as you talk together. Then recall the statement in the book: "This way of life makes sense and offers deep happiness *only if* you can discern the kingdom of heaven as a present reality and draw strength and encouragement from it while trusting God for its ultimate fulfillment." Discuss the factors that, in our present way of living, make it difficult to experience the kingdom of heaven as a present reality.

To close, hand each person a copy of the Beatitudes passage from Matthew 5:3-12. Read it aloud in unison. Suggest that they keep the copy in a prominent place during the coming week as a way of remembering that this way of life is possible even now—even today—through the life, death, and resurrection of Jesus Christ.

4. Jesus Changes "Outsiders" Into "Insiders"
Matthew 8–12

Faith Focus
Jesus' powerful actions demonstrate that the kingdom of heaven includes all who are willing to be included.

Before the Session
As you read Matthew 8–12, pay particular attention to the shift in focus from Jesus' sayings and teachings to Jesus' actions. Note the variety of people who meet Jesus and are changed by that encounter. Consider how Jesus' Sermon on the Mount in Matthew 5–7 lays the groundwork for and gives perspective and meaning to Jesus' healings in Matthew 8–12.

Claim Your Story
Call the group's attention to the "reality of inner rings of childhood friendships" discussed in "Claim Your Story." Invite participants to share a story from their own experience of being inside or outside a circle of friends. You may want to describe an experience of your own to get the conversation started.

What motivates people (or social systems) to create groups that inevitably exclude others? What factors push people to the margins of community?

When have you or someone close to you experienced being an outsider, living at the margins of a community or even a church congregation? What factors contributed to that situation?

Enter the Bible Story
Matthew 8–9
Invite the group to consider how Jesus' healings and miracles in Matthew 8–9 contribute to our understanding of him as the Christ who suffers and dies on a cross.

How do you think Jesus' miraculous deeds legitimize the authority of what he says?

In light of the responses by those who encountered Jesus, what does it mean for you, as a believer, to acknowledge Jesus' authority?

How would you answer the question that concludes the stilling of the storm passage in Matthew 8:27: "What sort of man is this, that even the winds and sea obey him?"

When Jesus encounters the paralytic in Matthew 9:2-8, he offers forgiveness first and then healing. When have you received from Jesus healing and forgiveness at the same time?

Matthew 10

Having showcased Jesus' authority in a flurry of healings and miraculous deeds, Matthew presents us with Jesus conferring that authority on his closest followers. With that authority "over unclean spirits, to cast them out, and to cure every disease and every sickness" (10:1), Jesus gives his disciples instruction and warning.

What is the main theme of Jesus' words of instructions to his disciples (10:5-15)? How do Jesus' instructions speak to your life of faith?

What is the main theme of Jesus' warning to his disciples (10:16-33)? When have you, as a Christian, felt like a sheep among wolves and in need of a word to speak in defense of your faith and received exactly what was needed?

Considering what Jesus says to his disciples in 10:32-42, how do you think he wanted their mission to be received?

How do you think you are supposed to respond to Jesus' statement: "Whoever loves father or mother more than me is not worthy of me"?

Matthew 11–12

John's query of Jesus, "Are you the one who is to come?" raises the issue of expectations, or how would-be followers of Jesus—even the most earnest ones—are inclined to fit him into their own preconceived expectations.

What do you think John wanted to see Jesus doing other than healing the blind, deaf, and lame?

Why would Jesus, in response to John's question, say, "Blessed is anyone who takes no offense at me?" What could be offensive about the message Jesus was proclaiming and the things he was doing? Who today is still offended by Jesus? When have you found yourself put off by Jesus' teaching?

Jesus placed himself in opposition to the restrictive interpretations of sabbath-keeping for what reason? How do you keep the sabbath and keep Jesus as Lord of it (12:8)?

Live the Story

Identify groups in your community that people typically want to belong to, and write these on a markerboard or a large sheet of paper. Once the list is compiled, discuss the factors or perceived benefits that make belonging to such groups so desirable and exclusion from such groups so disheartening.

Then identify the membership requirements of the community Jesus came to inaugurate. Discuss the benefits and risks of belonging to a Christian community today. Invite people to consider ways in which they might participate more fully in a Christian group or community in your local church.

To close, offer the following prayer or one of your own: Thank you, God, for extending open arms to us without condition. Give us courage to welcome others as you welcome us; in Christ we pray. Amen.

5. Jesus Proclaims the Kingdom of Heaven
Matthew 13–22

Faith Focus
The kingdom of heaven that Jesus describes can at times surprise and challenge, appeal to and threaten us.

Before the Session
One way to study this lengthy portion of Matthew is in sections. Chapter 13 contains a collection of Jesus' parables concerning the nature of God's kingdom (or the kingdom of heaven). What does Jesus want his followers to understand about that kingdom?

Chapters 14 and 17–18 offer glimpses of Jesus interacting with his disciples and using every opportunity to teach. What do the disciples learn from Jesus through the miraculous feeding; walking on water; the Transfiguration; and their conversations about faith, greatness, and forgiveness?

Finally, Chapters 15–16 and 19–22 reveal Jesus coming into conflict with the Pharisees and other religious leaders, setting the stage for his crucifixion. What puts Jesus at odds with religious authority?

Claim Your Story
Nearly everyone who encountered Jesus, from poorest peasant to closest disciple to educated scribe, found it difficult to grasp completely his message. The reason is probably simple: Jesus wasn't exactly what they were looking for, so they missed him. People still miss Jesus today. Talk together about your preconceived notions of Jesus that make it difficult, still today, to hear what he is saying.

When you hear the phrase *the kingdom of heaven*, what comes to mind: a place? a concept? a vision of the future? a way of living?

When Jesus describes the kingdom of heaven, how might your presuppositions prevent you from hearing what he is saying?

Enter the Bible Story
Matthew 13
The picture Jesus paints of the kingdom of heaven is surprising: like crops that grow according to the soil they are planted in, like a field that yields weeds and wheat side by side, like a hidden treasure or a priceless pearl, like a measure of yeast or the tiniest of seeds.

How do Jesus' parables in Matthew 13 challenge your understanding of the church's mission in today's world?

Which parable best describes how you see yourself participating in Jesus' work?

Matthew 14; 16:13-28; 17–18
Throughout these chapters, the disciples seem not to understand Jesus. Their first response to seeing hungry crowds is to send them away. Peter nearly drowns for lack of

faith. A few of them are concerned about which one will sit at Jesus' right hand. They can't even manage to cure a sick child.

When have you witnessed the presence of Christ so powerfully that your only response was like the disciples in the boat: "Truly you are the Son of God"?

Consider Peter's great confession of faith in 16:16. How have you experienced your faith in Christ as something you boldly proclaim but only halfheartedly live out?

How do you understand Jesus' instruction that "unless you become like little children, you will never enter the kingdom of heaven"?

Matthew 15–16:12; 19–22

Jesus unsettled the religious leaders of his day. Whether by saying when to wash your hands, whom to pay taxes to, who can get divorced, or why not to sell sacrificial doves in the Temple, Jesus took issue with the worship of God's law and instead proclaimed God's redemptive work among all people, especially the poor and the outcast.

When Jesus labels the Pharisees "hypocrites" (15:7) or play-actors, he is calling them to account for pretending to be pious. Where do you see evidence of pretended piety in your own life?

Jesus challenged religious traditions that had lost their connections to the real intentions of God's Word (Torah). What measures do you believe the church should take to keep its traditions grounded in Scripture?

Live the Story

According to Matthew's account, whenever Jesus taught in parables, spoke with his disciples, or argued with the Pharisees, he made clear that the way of life he was living and proclaiming came with rewards and requirements. Ask your group to think back over what Jesus said and taught in these chapters. Then discuss these questions:

How does your discipleship meet the requirements Jesus calls for?

What will you need to do to live out the gospel in a culture that glorifies material things and sees spiritual things only as a means to an end?

What priorities do you need to rearrange in your life to prepare you for the life Jesus calls for?

Will you make a public proclamation to ensure that you will do something to improve your discipleship?

6. How Do We Live for the Future Now?
Matthew 23–25

Faith Focus

Rather than wondering and worrying about the future, Jesus calls us to active waiting for the future that God will bring.

Before the Session

As you read these chapters, especially Chapter 24, don't get sidetracked by the vivid, end-of-the-age language and imagery you encounter. Consider consulting a basic commentary on this part of Matthew to help guide your reading and discussion. At the same time, keep in mind Jesus' key teachings in these chapters: We won't know the exact moment when the Son of Man returns; and while we wait, we need to do God's work of justice and mercy.

Consider bringing to the group session a stock report page from a newspaper to use as a visual prompt for the opening discussion.

Claim Your Story

Ask the group to think about the resources—financial and emotional—that they invest in securing their future, such as insurance, retirement savings, stocks, and education funds, as well as dieting, worrying, hoarding, and so on. Show a stock report page, and ask how many people regularly consult it. Then discuss together how people envision the future, particularly how the world will end.

What do you wish you could know about your future?

What worries you most about the future—your own, your children's, the world's?

When you hear the phrase *prepare for the future*, what does it call to mind?

Enter the Bible Story

Matthew 23

On occasion, Jesus uttered harsh words. This chapter recounts one of those occasions. Jesus condemned religious authorities for making religion too heavy a burden to bear.

Invite participants to read Jesus' seven "Woe to you" statements in Matthew 23. Ask them to rephrase each statement to describe issues or problems among today's religious authorities and church traditions. In other words, imagine what Jesus would say in critique of the church today. Finally, discuss this question: When have you experienced congregational life as a distraction to your faith life?

Matthew 24

God's future, like the experience of birthing a child, includes joy and pain, hope and uncertainty, expectation and surprise. The problem for most of us is that on one hand we try to live as if we can control that future, while on the other hand we try to figure out what God has in store. We can do neither, as Jesus succinctly reminded his followers.

What beliefs about "end times" are popular today? How do those popular ideas compare with what Jesus says in Matthew 24?

Do you ever think about the end of things? If so, how does it affect or inform your faith?

Matthew 25

Notice that the way Jesus talked about the new age to come (which he refered to as the kingdom of heaven) is to tell parables.

What does the parable of the ten bridesmaids tell you about how to live for the future now?

What does the parable of the talents say to you about how you are held accountable to put your faith into practice?

What does the parable of the sheep and goats tell you about your participation in God's future?

Live the Story

What we know about the future is, well, there is going to be one. That in itself is reassuring! We do know that God is concerned about the future, and God wants *us* to be concerned. Beyond that there are several important things to keep in mind.

First, we all have a part in creating the future. We are not simply inhabitants of this planet. We are its shapers and makers, and God will judge us accordingly.

Second, God expects us to influence the future by our care of those who are disadvantaged or marginalized by sickness, poverty, or perhaps even their sins.

Finally, it is not our business to know when the human story will end. Being ready—and getting the world ready—are our business.

What do you think "being ready" might look like in your daily living?

Consider one investment, financial or otherwise, that you can make in God's future that you are not currently making. What would it take for you to make that investment?

7. The Abandonment of Jesus the Messiah
Matthew 26:1-27:31a

Faith Focus
Even knowing that we will disappoint, fail, and sometimes abandon him, Jesus never stops loving us.

Before the Session
Matthew's Passion narrative—that is, the account of Jesus' last hours before his crucifixion and burial—begins in Chapter 26. As you read, keep your eyes on Jesus, of course, but don't miss the interaction of those who encounter Jesus on his way to the cross. You may see yourself in one of them.

Create a poster–sized collage of images of Jesus during his last hours: eating with the disciples, praying at Gethsemane, on trial before Pilate, being mocked and whipped by soldiers, wearing the crown of thorns, and so on. Most can be found online and printed on a color printer. Use the poster as a meditation visual for the close of the session.

Claim Your Story
The opening question posed in our reading is simply worded: What kind of disciple are you? As we read these final chapters of Jesus' story, another question arises: What kind of Lord do we follow? Both questions pursue us all through our Christian lives. Take time to go around the group and hear responses to those two questions. Consider two other questions to further your discussion:

What do you believe Christ expects of you?

How do you protect yourself from the possibility that you will deny, betray, or run away from Christ as the disciples did?

Enter the Bible Story
Matthew 26:1-35
The events that take place in these verses are full of meaning. A woman spills oil on Jesus' feet. Jesus breaks bread among friends who will soon desert him. Both events foreshadow his impending death.

Despite their years of following Jesus, the disciples were neither sure of themselves nor sure of Jesus. When have you doubted your belief in Jesus?

How might your understanding of Jesus' teachings at the Last Supper give meaning to your experience of Holy Communion?

Matthew 26:36-75
From the moment Jesus arrived in the garden of Gethsemane, he was walking to his death. Pay attention to what Jesus did, said, and didn't say on this journey.

What does Jesus' prayer at Gethsemane say to you about his relationship with God? How might it inform your prayers to God?

When we hear Peter deny Christ, we can't help but remember his confession of Jesus as the Messiah. What does Matthew want his readers to think of Peter in this chapter? What does Matthew want his readers to think of themselves?

Matthew 27:1-31a

Jesus' final confrontation with religious and political leaders is a conflict between two motivations: the love of power and the power of love. At that moment, the love of power seemed to have the advantage, for Jesus was condemned to die.

Jesus challenged the religious and political status quo of his day. How does he still do that in our day?

Have you ever had to stand up for the truth of Christ in the face of powerful opposition? When have you felt that your faith was on trial?

What do you make of the fact that just as an innocent Jesus was condemned, a guilty criminal was pardoned?

Live the Story

How do you respond to this portion of Jesus' story?

To help participants form a response to the question, point out that images of Jesus during his last hours—agonizing in a garden, standing with head bowed before Pilate and bound to a whipping post, wearing a crown of thorns—have been expressed by artists for centuries. To illustrate, display the poster collage of images of Jesus described above.

Invite the group to reflect in silence on these images of Jesus and on their own mental picture of Jesus as he made his way toward the cross. After an appropriate length of time, invite group members to share, in a sentence or two, what Jesus' death means for them. Finally, pose this question: How does Jesus death inform the way you live?

8. The Death and Resurrection of Jesus
Matthew 27:31b–28:20

Faith Focus
The kingdom of heaven and the love of God shown in Jesus Christ are not limited by sin or death.

Before the Session
Matthew's account of Jesus' death, burial, and resurrection is loaded with drama. The sky grows dark. Jesus cries out in anguish. The Temple curtain rips. Graves burst open. Bystanders plunge into the action. People wail in the distance. The earth trembles. A huge stone rolls away from an empty tomb. Why so dramatic? What is Matthew up to here? This is the beginning of the end, in a way: the end of sin and death. Be sure to convey to your group that seeing the poignancy of these last verses is crucial in understanding the great commission that we as the church have been given. Christ is risen! The Kingdom is here! Go tell it on a mountain!

Have on hand copies of the Apostles' Creed and hymnals for use during the close of the session. Be sure the hymnals include "When I Survey the Wondrous Cross."

Assemble a collection of cross photos or art or perhaps a variety of crosses containing jewelry, wall crosses, and other representations. Ask participants what crosses they have in their homes.

Claim Your Story
The death of a Jewish teacher at the hands of the Romans in first-century Palestine hardly seems newsworthy. Yet since that event, the world has never been the same. Talk together about how your life, values, decisions, language, and worldview have been influenced by the story of Jesus. Invite group members to answer this question: Why does the crucified and risen Jesus matter in the twenty-first century?

Enter the Bible Story
Matthew 27:31b-66
Jesus' crucifixion was a unique and iconic moment in human history. As such, one way to approach a discussion of it is to focus on some of those who witnessed the event.

Simon of Cyrene. How do you imagine Simon reacted when forced to shoulder Jesus' crossbeam? How do you think he recalled the event later? When have you been given a cross to carry that you didn't expect? How did you manage it?

The Centurion. What do you think Matthew intends his readers to see in the centurion's statement: "Truly, this man was God's Son"? When you have looked squarely at the reality of a crucified Jesus, what words come to you?

Mary Magdalene. By the time Jesus breathed his last, the only followers remaining near the cross were several women, including Mary Magdalene. What do you think motivated her and the other women to maintain their vigil at the cross? What keeps you near Christ even when he appears to the world to be weak and vulnerable?

Matthew 28

On that first Easter morning, an angel announced the news of Jesus' resurrection to the women at the tomb. First, he told them not to be afraid. Second, he redirected the focus from the cross to the empty tomb. Third, he said to run and tell others. Finally, he promised that Jesus would meet them where they were going. Use those four elements of the angel's speech to discuss a proper response to Jesus' resurrection today.

To what extent do the radical and risky implications of believing in Jesus' resurrection scare you? How?

As told in Matthew, which is the more troublesome to comprehend: Jesus' crucifixion or his resurrection?

When have you told someone the story of Jesus? Was it easy or hard for you to do? What was the response of the one you told?

When have you felt the presence of the risen Christ?

Live the Story

As we are reminded in the book, this portion of Matthew is not a story to be read, enjoyed, and then laid aside. Nor is it one simply to be discussed and speculated upon. For those who will receive it—that is, those who are willing to accept its message and become disciples—Matthew's record is a compelling call. Go around the group discussing how the experience of studying Matthew has informed or invigorated your call to discipleship.

To close, distribute copies of the Apostles' Creed and lead your group in reciting it together as an act of recommitment to the gospel message. Then, as a closing prayer, recite or sing the hymn "When I Survey the Wondrous Cross."

CPSIA information can be obtained
at www.ICGtesting.com
Printed in the USA
LVOW12s0208170616
492881LV00001BC/1/P

9 781426 709821